Twayne's English Authors Series

Sylvia E. Bowman, *Editor*

INDIANA UNIVERSITY

John Dryden

 14

John Dryden

By GEORGE R. WASSERMAN

Russell Sage College

Twayne Publishers, Inc. :: New York

For
My
Parents

Preface

The influence of twentieth-century criticism upon the taste
and interests of undergraduate students of English literature
and the excitement which a generation ago made today's
teachers admirers of Metaphysical and, later, of Augustan poetry
have only recently begun to touch Dryden. Never forgotten—as
the well-read pages of surviving volumes of Scott's edition
testify—Dryden has nevertheless long existed as our best example
of the poet's or historian's poet, as the critic's critic. No serious
student would have hesitated to place him as a figure of the
first importance, but most would have had to acknowledge a
literary history as the authority for their judgment, their survey
courses having failed to "get to him" in the first semester, yet
assuming him "covered" in the second. This attitude of cool
respectability was at least partially due to his having been
elevated only nominally in the present century's revaluation of
seventeenth-century literature, for Dryden's peculiar facility or
"wit" of allusion remained beyond the scope of "close reading"
until that critical instrument became itself sensitized to the
allusiveness of Augustan literature. Curiously, Dryden, who was
Pope's teacher, has had to wait for the current reassimilation of his
disciple for his own rediscovery.

The appearance in 1956 of the first volume of the California
Edition of Dryden's complete works marks the beginning of
what I believe is a new enthusiasm for Dryden. To assist his
editors, a concordance and a new (and certain to be standard)
biography have appeared; and, to serve until their task is completed, we have been given a more than adequate British
edition of the complete poems and verse translations, and reissues
of both Ker's edition of the essays and the still indispensable

Life by Scott. The results of this activity, the reexamination of every area of the poet's work, are already evident in an increasing number of publications, only a small part of which can be dealt with in the pages to follow.

The aim of this book is accordingly modest; it does not attempt to synthesize or even to review the current scholarship on Dryden. It will try, if possible, to convey to the reader unfamiliar with Dryden the new enthusiasm for the poet which I believe characterizes this scholarship. Owing to the necessity of detailed analysis and quotation, I have had to be selective within the major areas of Dryden's work—early poems, criticism, drama, satire, religious poems, and translations; the opening biographical chapter attempts to provide a more comprehensive survey of his total output. It is hoped, however, that the interested reader will himself supply my omissions.

Acknowledgment of my own indebtedness to many Dryden scholars—both old and new—must be deferred to the footnotes and bibliography at the end of this volume. It is a pleasure to acknowledge here, however, my gratitude to Dr. Lewis A. Froman, for a grant during the summer of 1963; to Dr. Virginia Radley and my colleagues in the English Department for cheerfully assuming the additional burdens entailed by my reduced teaching load; and to my wife, for encouragement and assistance far beyond the call of duty.

GEORGE R. WASSERMAN

Russell Sage College

Contents

Chronology

1631   John Dryden born August 9, in the vicarage of Aldwinkle All Saints.

1649   First published poem, an elegy on the death of Henry, Lord Hastings, appeared in *Lachrymae Musarum*.

1650-   Dryden in residence at Trinity College, Cambridge.
1654

1659   "Heroique Stanzas to the Glorious Memory of Cromwell" published with eulogies by Waller and Sprat in *Three Poems upon the Death of his late Highness Oliver Lord Protector of England, Scotland, and Ireland*.

1660   *Astraea Redux* published on the return of Charles II.

1663   *The Wild Gallant*, Dryden's first play, produced. December 1, married to Lady Elizabeth Howard.

1665   *The Indian Emperor* produced. June, theaters closed by outbreak of bubonic plague; the Drydens flee to Wiltshire, where they remain at least until November, 1666.

1667   *Annus Mirabilis* published; *Secret Love* produced.

1668   April, Dryden made Poet Laureate at the death of Sir William Davenant; becomes exclusive writer for the Theatre Royal; *An Essay of Dramatic Poesy* published.

1669   *Tyrannic Love* produced.

1670-   *Conquest of Granada*, Parts I and II produced. George
1671   Villiers' *The Rehearsal* produced. *Marriage à la Mode* probably produced by end of 1671.

1672   January, Theatre Royal destroyed by fire.

1674   March, new Theatre Royal in Drury Lane opened.

1675   *Aureng-Zebe* produced.

1677   *All for Love* produced.

1678   September, Titus Oates "exposes" details of the Popish Plot. Dryden breaks with the Theatre Royal; Jacob Tonson becomes his publisher.

1679   Dryden's earliest translations published in a collection of Ovid's *Epistles*.

1681   March 21, Charles dissolves the third Oxford Parliament and puts an end to Whig attempts to pass the Exclusion Bill. July, Shaftesbury awaits trial in the Tower; November, *Absalom and Achitophel* published.

1682   March, *The Medall* published. May, Shadwell's *The Medal of John Bayes* published; October, pirated edition of *Mac Flecknoe* published; November, *Religio Laici* published.

1684   Dryden authorizes publication of *Mac Flecknoe* in the first of Tonson's Miscellanies.

1685   February 6, Charles II dies; accession of James II; Dryden becomes a Catholic. "To the Memory of Anne Killigrew" published.

1687   April 4, King James' Declaration of Indulgence. *The Hind and the Panther* and "A Song for St. Cecilia's Day" published.

1688   June, birth of a son to King James II celebrated in *Britannia Rediviva*. December, James vacates the throne; William and Mary crowned.

1689   Dryden's return to the theater marked by the production of *Don Sebastian*.

1693   *Satires of Juvenal and Persius* published, prefaced by "A Discourse concerning . . . Satire."

1697   *The Works of Virgil* and "Alexander's Feast" published.

1700   *The Fables* published. May 1, death of Dryden.

John Dryden

CHAPTER 1

Life and Times

A note in the seventeenth-century biographer John Aubrey's *Brief Lives* reads: "John Dreyden, esq., Poet Laureate. He will write it for me Himselfe."[1] One wonders if the century's greatest collector of gossip had at last met his match in a subject whose renown served only to conceal his personality, and who remarked in a rare moment of self-revelation—"My conversation is slow and dull; my humour saturnine and reserved; in short, I am none of those who endeavour to break jests in company, or make reparties [sic]."[2] Congreve, Dryden's younger contemporary and literary executor, corroborates this picture in his dedication to Dryden's *Dramatic Works* (1717); and he adds that "he had something in his nature, that abhorred intrusion into any society whatsoever." Such remarks—along with Pope's recollection that Dryden "employed his morning in writing; dined, *en famille*; and then went to Wills': only he came home earlier a' nights," and Malone's memory of the aged poet's summer and winter seats at that coffee house—constitute the seemingly insignificant characterizing detail on which biography partly depends;[3] but, excepting the possibly libelous rumors circulated by his enemies, Dryden left his biographers little of himself outside his works. Apparently, he failed to write his "life" for Aubrey; but the two sentences after his name in the *Brief Lives* are not an unfitting epitaph to the professional man of letters whose career we are about to sketch.

We are, moreover, not much better supplied with the factual substance of Dryden's life, whose first twenty years are not more thoroughly documented than the corresponding years of his ancestors' lives—though, since the families of both his father and mother were of some distinction, this is not surprising. Since the sixteenth century both families had held extensive lands in Northamptonshire: the Drydens in Canons Ashby, the

Pickerings in Tichmarsh. Both, too, were apparently of Puritan convictions, and the offspring of an earlier alliance between them was to become Oliver Cromwell's Lord Chamberlain, Sir Gilbert Pickering. Not far from Tichmarsh, in the vicarage of Aldwinkle All Saints, where his maternal grandfather, the Reverend Henry Pickering was rector, John Dryden, the first of fourteen children to Erasmus and Mary Dryden, was born on August 9, 1631.[4] Here, it is likely, he spent his earliest years, possibly attending, as a tablet in the Tichmarsh Church claims, the village grammar school.[5] Certainly, however, he went on to Westminster School in London as a King's Scholar, submitting to that fierce regimen of Latin and Greek which produced so many illustrious men of letters, and to the ferrule of Dr. Richard Busby, "to whom," Dryden later reported, "I am not only oblig'd my self, for the best part of my own Education, and that of my two Sons; but have also receiv'd from him the first and truest Taste of *Persius.*"[6]

Clearly, too, he had begun to write verse by this time, for his contribution in 1649 to a collection of elegies on the death of Henry, Lord Hastings, *Lachrymae Musarum: The Tears of the Muses,* took its place not only with the productions of five other Westminster boys, but with those of such established poets as Herrick, Marvell, and Denham. With the distinction of a published poem and a Westminster scholarship, Dryden entered Trinity College, Cambridge in 1650. Shortly after his admittance he again appeared in print, this time in a slight commendatory poem prefacing a volume of religious epigrams, *Sion and Parnassus,* published in 1650 by John Hoddesdon, a young man Dryden may have known at Westminster or at Cambridge.[7] This first phase of his career came to an end in 1654 when, possibly as a consequence of his father's death in that year, he took his baccalaureate and concluded his residence at the university.

I 1654-1678

It is not known whether Dryden, twenty-three years old at that time, returned home to assume the responsibilities of his inheritance, or sought out his kinsman Sir Gilbert Pickering in London, to gain employment in Cromwell's government. The appearance in 1659 of his "Heroique Stanzas to . . . Cromwell" does not necessarily strengthen the second possibility. Perhaps the most significant mark of this poem, aside from its overall evidence of the author's maturity, is its discriminating praise of the man as distinct from his party. The occasion certainly offered an opportunity to court Parliamentary favor, but Dryden seems either to have been (to say the worst) too shrewd an analyst of the party's future to wish to link his reputation to it, or he was simply unsympathetic with its cause. Clearly Cromwell's death provided Dryden with an occasion which warranted poetic commentary of an heroic nature, a poetic species which attached little importance to the expression of sincere feeling. In view of the great value which, throughout his career, he placed upon the heroic poem, it should not be surprising to find him engaged in it whenever an opportunity presented itself. His enemies, however, never allowed Charles' Poet Laureate to forget this tribute; they took special delight in later reprinting it, once (1681) altering its title to *An Elegy on the Usurper O. C. by the Author of Absalom and Achitophel, published to show the Loyalty and Integrity of the Poet.* His most judicious biographer, moreover, has rejected for want of adequate evidence the supposition that Dryden held a minor political job under Cromwell.[8]

Nor is there much better evidence that he worked at this time for the bookseller Henry Herringman, though this connection is generally assumed in view of the inclusion of the unknown poet's "Heroique Stanzas" along with the poems of Edmund Waller and Thomas Sprat in *Three Poems upon the Death of his late Highness Oliver Cromwell . . .*, a collection which was originally Herringman's venture. An association with Herringman might also account for Dryden's early relationship with Sir Robert Howard, one who would soon play an important role in the poet's professional and private life. In 1660, Herringman published a collection of the nobleman's works, to which Dryden contributed a commendatory poem, fulsome in its praise of Howard's literary qualifications, but nevertheless significant as the earliest expression of Dryden's royalism. His tribute to Howard as the "brave captain" who restores poesie to her rightful throne of "Morall Knowledge" is paralleled in this poem by a reference to the recent success of General Monck in restoring Charles to his; Howard's volume is thus "happy in its Geniture:

/For since 'tis born when *Charles* ascends the Throne,/It shares at once his Fortune and its own."⁹

Dryden's praise of Howard's verse as the sign of a Golden Age of Poetry inspired by King Charles' return was no doubt merely a pretty compliment to the poet's patriotism. That Dryden conceived of a very real relation between this event and his own poetic fortunes, however, is suggested by the works in which he was next engaged: *Astraea Redux*, a celebration of "the happy Restoration and return" of Charles II, in May 1660; *To His Sacred Majesty*, a coronation panegyric, in the following year; and on New Year's Day, 1662, the verses addressed to the Lord Chancellor, Edward Hyde. All three poems cover the conventional topics of praise dictated by formal compliment, but here, as was not true in the panegyric to Cromwell, the praise of the man is tantamount to an endorsement of his politics. In theme and structure, the poems themselves demonstrate the poet's commitment to the principle of monarchy as an all-inclusive value and order.

This partisanship was also given dramatic expression in an attempted tragedy about the Duke of Guise. In *Astraea Redux*, Dryden referred to the parallel between the adversities of Charles II and his grandfather Henry IV of France, both of whom were oppressed by "Covenanting leagues," and, as he later wrote, the recognition of the similarities between the French Holy League and the Presbyterian Solemn League seemed "the Fairest way," in 1660, "of setting forth the *Rise* of the *Late Rebellion;* and by *Exploding* the Villanies of it upon the *Stage,* to *Precaution Posterity* against the Like *Errors.*"¹⁰ The play was left unfinished on the advice of friends who objected to its artlessness, but the scene in blank verse of the Duke's return to Paris ("taken *Verbatim* out of Davila," the contemporary historian of France's civil wars) survives in a later tragedy called *The Duke of Guise* (1682), a collaborative effort with Nathaniel Lee.

Dryden also foresaw a new age of science in the Restoration of Charles—who would, in 1663, bestow his patronage upon the recently chartered Royal Society. His verses "To my Honour'd Friend Dr. Charleton," prefixed to Charleton's archeological tract on Stonehenge and published in 1663, make therefore much the same claim for the natural scientist and philosopher as those to Howard had made for the poet. The reference to Charleton as a "friend" may help to explain his nomination of Dryden for membership in the Royal Society in the same year,[11] a fact which does not however imply that the latter had more than a poet's interest in science. It was no doubt as a man of letters that Dryden was elected to the Society, for, in the three years before he was dropped from its rolls for nonpayment of fees, we know only of his having served with the poet Waller (and possibly Abraham Cowley) on a committee appointed to improve the language, a matter of which the scientists were solicitous, if only, as Thomas Sprat puts it in his *History* of the Society, to prevent "the whole spirit and vigour of their *Design*" from being "soon eaten out, by the luxury and redundance of speech."[12]

To what extent their endorsement of literary simplicity and clarity contributed to these virtues in Dryden's own writing is difficult to determine; a remark he later made in the "Defense of an Essay of Dramatic Poesy" (1668), indicates, however, another way in which he was influenced by the Society. Defending himself there against Sir Robert Howard's allegation of critical dogmatism in the *Essay*, Dryden calls attention to that disinterested and antidogmatic approach to differing literary views which takes the form of dialogue in his work; and he remarks that "my whole discourse was sceptical, according to that way of reasoning which . . . is imitated by the modest inquisitions of the Royal Society."[13] However slight, then, Dryden's contact with the Society was important insofar as it nurtured that natural disinterest and scepticism which is the most characteristic quality of his critical writing and, later, of his religious thought.

Dryden's apparent optimism about his literary future in the reign of King Charles rested partially at least upon the King's well-known love of the theater, and indeed within a matter of months after the coronation, patents were issued to Thomas Killigrew and Sir William Davenant to form two companies of players and to erect two theaters, thereafter known as the King's Theatre or Theatre Royal, and the Duke's Theatre, in view of the respective patronage of Charles and of James, Duke of York.[14] Among the important investors of capital in the King's Company was Sir Robert Howard, with whom Dryden had become better acquainted since his earlier literary relationship; and it was probably Howard's connection which formed Dryden's early association with this company.

That he would very likely have turned to the theatre even without such a connection however, is suggested by his earlier projected tragedy on the Duke of Guise; and at some time in 1662, he seriously returned his attention in this direction, producing early in the next year a comedy called *The Wild Gallant*, and collaborating with Howard on *The Indian Queen*, which appeared at the beginning of 1664. *The Wild Gallant*, Dryden later remarked in the preface to the published version, was condemned by "the greater part" of the town, he himself offering no other excuse for it than its being no worse nor more incorrect than other plays then receiving applause. *The Indian Queen* created a sensation, however, partly because of its use of elaborate scenery and costumes—a factor which now set the King's Company in more equal competition with its rival—and partly as an example of the French styled, rhyming tragedy favored by the king. We may assume that Dryden's part in this success (which is conjectured to be at least equal to if not greater than his collaborator's)[15] is an indication of Howard's respect for the poet's abilities.

At the time of the first performance, however, the relationship between the two men was no longer merely professional, for a month earlier (in December, 1663) Dryden had married Howard's sister, Lady Elizabeth. She came to him—or so tradition has it—under the cloud of some personal disgrace, to which an enemy might still allude twenty years later in an attack upon her then distinguished poet-husband;[16] but evidence either to substantiate or to disprove the accusations has not survived. The marriage appears not to have been materially advantageous to Dryden—nor, according to Sir Walter Scott, even compatible. In one of the most sharply worded pages of his *Life* of the poet, Scott dismisses what is called a "disagreeable subject" with the observation that "on no one occasion, when a sarcasm against matrimony could be introduced, has our author failed to season it with such bitterness, as spoke an inward consciousness of domestic misery."[17] But even if the reputation of Lady Elizabeth was somewhat tarnished, that of her noble family was not; and Dryden's alliance with it may at least be interpreted as evidence, at this stage of his career, of his promise as a writer of distinction.

Dryden's second independent dramatic effort, *The Rival Ladies*, was apparently begun not long after the appearance of *The Wild Gallant*, though it was not produced until after *The Indian Queen*. Anxious, no doubt, to avoid the mistakes of his first play, Dryden now combined with his comic action (the most difficult kind of drama, he believed) scenes and characters designed to engage the audience's concern; a further appeal for acceptance was made by his choice of Spanish materials which were enjoying some vogue at this time. But the success for which he hoped arrived only with his next play, *The Indian Emperor*, a sequel to his collaboration with Howard; and, like that, a tragedy on love and honor in heroic rhyme. Unfortunately, even this success could hardly have proven itself before an outbreak of bubonic plague in the spring of 1665 sharply curtailed theater attendance and in June altogether shut down the playhouses. With thousands of others, Dryden and his wife fled the city, taking residence at his father-in-law's estate at Charlton in Wiltshire. That he was still there in November of the following year is indicated by the signature of the dedicatory letter to his brother-in-law, prefacing *Annus Mirabilis,* a work with which Dryden was probably engaged in the latter months of this retirement, since two of the events celebrated in the poem—the imminent naval victory of the English over the Dutch, and the great fire of London—occurred in the summer of 1666. The earlier months were probably spent in those reflections upon the art of drama which formed the substance of *An Essay of Dramatic Poesy;* and, since the prefatory letter to Sir Robert also makes reference to a play "not long since" sent to Howard for his inspection, *Secret Love*—Dryden's next play to appear— was probably written at this time.

The dedication of *Annus Mirabilis* and the felicitous relations between Dryden and Howard which it implies indicate the purely literary character of the "quarrel" between the two men which, since the end of 1664, had begun to attract public attention. At that time, Dryden had made the dedication of *The Rival Ladies* to Roger Boyle, Earl of Orrery, the occasion for an essay in defense of rhyme in serious drama, a practice which had been followed by Orrery and, in the serious scenes of *The Rival*

Ladies and *The Indian Queen,* by Dryden. At the beginning of the next year, Howard prefaced a collection of four of his plays with an essay which condemned the use of rhyme in tragedy, notwithstanding his own part in the composition of *The Indian Queen.* By 1668, Dryden had himself laid aside, as "troublesome and slow," this practice, but he still approved of it in principle. He had restated his defense of rhyme in Neander's dispute with Crites at the end of the *Essay of Dramatic Poesy.* As his dedication of the *Essay* to Lord Buckhurst indicates, Dryden would probably have preferred to let the issue rest there, and the problematic treatment of ideas in the *Essay* may have seemed the best means of doing so. Howard, however, appears not to have understood the work in this way, for in the preface to *The Duke of Lerma,* published shortly after the *Essay* in June, 1668, he misrepresents Dryden's arguments and accuses him of having been dictatorial in that work. Reluctantly, but in the harshest terms yet employed by either disputant, Dryden retaliated in the same year with "A Defence of an Essay of Dramatic Poesy," prefixed to the second edition of *The Indian Queen.* Since the "Defence" includes both ridicule of Howard's ungrammatical Latin and English and an accusation of his plagiarism in *The Duke of Lerma,* Dryden's obvious irritation might well be expected to have caused a rift in the relations with his brother-in-law, but there is evidence of a conciliatory spirit in Dryden's later suppression of the preface and in Howard's continuing interest in the poet's financial affairs.

In the busy months following his return from Wiltshire, probably early in 1667, Dryden's literary eminence was established. He had first no doubt to find housing in the fire-ravaged city for his wife and his son Charles, who was not yet a year old. (Two more sons, John and Erasmus, would be born in the next two years.)[18] The works composed at Wiltshire were to be readied for the stage and the press, *Annus Mirabilis* appearing early in 1667,[19] *Secret Love* (an immediate favorite of the king) shortly after it, and the *Essay of Dramatic Poesy* in the following year. Again in 1667, he adapted the Duke of Newcastle's translation of Molière's *L'Etourdi* as the popular farce *Sir Martin Mar-All,* and he assisted Sir William Davenant, the current Poet Laureate and the manager of the Duke's Company, in rendering Shakespeare's *The Tempest* as a Restoration musical comedy. In view of this association, and of his avowed admiration of the Laureate in the staunchly Stuart *Annus Mirabilis,* Dryden's election in April, 1668, to the post left vacant at Davenant's death seems not unexpected: nor was the decision of the managers of the Theatre Royal to offer Dryden at this time a share in the company's profits unrelated to the fact that both *Sir Martin Mar-All* and *The Tempest* had been given to their competitors. Dryden no doubt eagerly consented to an arrangement which assured him of "three or four hundred pounds" annually in exchange for giving the Theatre Royal exclusive rights to three new plays in the same period,[20] and he promptly offered the bright comedy *An Evening's Love* for production in the summer of 1668. In no year, however, was he to fulfill his part of the bargain, his total output in the next five years amounting to only seven plays.

Not until ten years later, when Dryden offered a play to the rival company, did the managers of the Theatre Royal lodge a formal complaint about these contractual violations. Dryden's name alone, distinguished now by the laureateship and in 1670 by the additional title of Historiographer Royal, was probably an important property; and, notwithstanding his delinquencies, the always difficult affiliation of artist and businessman seems to have been mutually satisfactory, at least at the beginning. Indeed, Charles Ward states that the great popularity of his next play, the heroic tragedy *Tyrannic Love* (his only production for 1669), "justified the action of the company in taking Dryden in on equal terms" with its leading actors.[21] In this play, and, the next two years, in *The Conquest of Granada,* a heroic tragedy in two parts, and the delightful and intelligent tragicomedy, *Marriage à la Mode,* Dryden for his part provided the King's Players with notable successes.

He had by now become the chief exponent of the rhymed heroic tragedy, and had done much in his own four examples to make the type popular—so popular, in fact, that in 1671 the King's Company felt it could afford to ridicule both it and their leading playwright in the production of *The Rehearsal* by George Villiers, Duke of Buckingham. This dramatic parody portrays Dryden as Bayes, a silly author of heroic drama who explains to two gentlemen the composition and workings of a new play supposedly in rehearsal. A clever pastiche of the mannerisms of the new-fashioned drama—its stock scenes of battle and of wit; its heavy reliance upon spectacle, machines, song and dance; and of course its rhyme and characteristic rhetoric—the parody debases at the same time some memorable passages of Dryden's and Howard's plays. Bayes' explanation is a satirical exposure not only of Dryden's professional mannerisms, particularly as revealed in his critical writings, but also of his personal habits of speech and dress. Dryden cannot have helped laughing, along with the rest of London's playgoers, at parts of *The Rehearsal;* it is also likely that there was much in it that offended him. Perhaps because of Buckingham's political power he forebore retaliating until, ten years later, the nobleman was in opposition to the king's policies; then Dryden took what he described as his greatest pleasure as a satirist in portraying him as Zimri in *Absalom and Achitophel.*

The Rehearsal probably did not, even momentarily, cause Dryden any misgivings about his course thus far in the theater. It has been suggested that, because it was not among the plays parodied, *Marriage à la Mode* was written after the production of Buckingham's farce, and was altered as a tragi-comedy in respect of the recent criticism of serious drama. Charles Ward, however, argues for a performance of the play before the end of 1671, and both the contemporary author of a "Key" to *The Rehearsal* and Sir Walter Scott believe that the latter does allude to *Marriage à la Mode.*[22] Buckingham's parody was more likely to have been, as George Saintsbury believed, an "advertisement" of heroic plays;[23] and, if Dryden was not to write another until 1675, there are probably other reasons to explain the fact. One was the immediate need to conciliate public resentment of the king's declaration of war against the Dutch in March, 1672—possibly an official duty of the Historiographer Royal which Dryden unhappily combined with his obligation to the Theatre Royal. The result was *Amboyna,* a tragedy (historical rather than heroic) memorializing the Dutch massacre of the London Company in 1623, and certainly Dryden's poorest play. Another reason for fewer heroic plays was the disastrous fire which in January, 1672, destroyed the Theatre Royal and with it the elaborate scenery and costumes upon which heroic tragedy so heavily depended. The company was forced to move to Lisle's Tennis Court (which had just been vacated by

its rival, now happily ensconced in Dorset Garden), and for the
sake of economy to revive old plays which Dryden was called
upon to update with a timely prologue or epilogue. *The Assignation*, a new and no doubt hastily written tragicomedy which he
probably offered in 1672, was hardly engaging enough to com-
pensate for these inconveniences.

The difficulties of competing with the now flourishing Duke's
Company increased during the two years in which the new
Theatre Royal was being rebuilt. As indicated by the prologues
and epilogues which Dryden wrote during these months, the
novelty of a French and an Italian troupe of players in London
reduced even further the dwindling audiences of the King's
Players and created a new taste for extravagance with which
Dryden would not and his theater could not comply. Even when
the new house in Drury Lane opened on March 26, 1674, the
stigma of the second-rate was not removed, as Dryden acknowledged in the prologue he wrote for the occasion:

> A Plain Built House after so long a stay,
> Will send you half unsatisfy'd away;
> When, fal'n from your expected Pomp, you find
> A bare convenience only is design'd;

but he unhappily rationalizes that

> 'Twere Folly now a stately Pile to raise,
> To build a Play-House while You throw down Plays.
> Whilst Scenes, Machines, and empty *Opera's* reign,
> And for the Pencil You the Pen disdain. (11. 1-4, 34-37)

The bitterness of Dryden's reference to opera reflects his chagrin
at the foreign players who helped to create the current taste for
theatrical extravaganza and at the Duke's Theatre which, since
Davenant's *The Siege of Rhodes* (1656), had long been closely
associated with the opera. In February, 1673, it had produced
Davenant's operatic version of *Macbeth*, and just one month after
the opening of the Drury Lane Theatre it staged Shadwell's
opera *The Tempest*. Quite possibly, as Charles Ward conjectures,
the Theatre Royal may have prevailed upon Dryden to write
an opera to celebrate this opening, and he may have complied
with his *The State of Innocence*, a reworking in rhyme, contain-
ing operatic sequences, of *Paradise Lost*.[24] The work was never
produced, however, perhaps because its production costs were

prohibitive or because it was felt that its subject would not "take," a view which might explain Dryden's reference to the "empty" operas then popular. Not until late in 1675, when the heroic tragedy *Aureng-Zebe* appeared, did Dryden contribute another play to the new house.

Disenchanted, then, with the current state of the theater and perhaps somewhat dissatisfied with his own dramatic work, Dryden appears at this time to have been giving more and more thought to the composition of a heroic poem of epic proportions. Heroic poetry had always been a matter of collateral interest in his work, and, since his preface to *Annus Mirabilis*, was touched upon in many of the prefaces and dedications of his plays; in the 1670's, this interest was probably intensified by his encounter with the important critical work of Rapin and Le Bossu.[25] His dedication of *Aureng-Zebe* (1676) to John Sheffield, Earl of Mulgrave, provides evidence that this interest in the epic was, however, not merely theoretical, for he speaks of making "the world some part of amends, for many ill Playes, by an Heroique Poem." His lordship "has been long acquainted" with the design, and had earlier helped to promote it by giving the poet "the opportunity of discoursing it to his Majesty, and his Royal Highness," both of whom, he adds, "were then pleas'd both to commend the Design, and to encourage it by their Commands."[26] They had apparently provided no financial encouragement, however, and it was this oversight which Dryden was now hoping to rectify with his graceful reference to Mulgrave as "a *Mecenas*." Royal interest in the project may have been expressed in a warrant for an additional one hundred pound annuity issued to the poet some months later in 1677,[27] a time, however, in which Charles was finding it increasingly difficult to meet his previously contracted obligations. Indeed, Dryden was lucky to receive even partial payment on his annual Laureate's pension of two hundred pounds, which was continually in arrears. This may have been the fate of the King's interest in the epic, for we hear nothing more of the project until 1693 when Dryden remarks that "being encouraged only with fair words by King Charles II, my little salary ill paid, and no prospect of a future subsistence." he was "discouraged in the beginning" of the attempt.[28]

In the meantime, his own financial difficulties forced him to continue writing for the theater, and in the next three years he produced five plays. The first of these, *All for Love* (1677)—an imitation in blank verse of Shakespeare's *Antony and Cleopatra* —is still Dryden's most admired play, and a financial success for the author, who was given "as a guift" the proceeds of *a third day's* presentation. This gesture was described as "a particular kindnesse of the Company," made in recognition of Dryden's complaint that since the burning of the theater his earnings had fallen "much short of what they were." We learn of these facts from a formal complaint of the managers of the King's Company to the Lord Chamberlain, charging that Dryden had not only failed to supply the company with the contracted three plays annually, but had recently offered a new tragedy, *Oedipus* (written with Nathaniel Lee) to the Duke's Company.[29] It is not known whether the plaintives received compensation for Dryden's breach of contract, but the charges cited suggest that the playwright foresaw the imminent bankruptcy of the King's Company, and, driven by his own financial need, turned to the rival theater as the means of enhancing the drawing power of his plays. The complaint, however, marks his complete break with the Theatre Royal. In 1679, the Duke's Company produced both *Oedipus* and *Troilus and Cressida*, another Shakespearean "improvement;" and, in the spring of 1680, the tragicomedy *The Spanish Friar* appeared under the same auspices.[30]

With *The Spanish Friar* Dryden's most active period in the theater ends. As a Tory propagandist, he would yet produce with Lee in 1682 *The Duke of Guise;* but not until 1685 would he return as a professional dramatist, and then to the United Companies, the formation of which from the two original companies in 1682 was only one of the effects of the political unrest of which Dryden was now to become the most inspired commentator.

II *1678-1685*

The series of events which prompted—or rather provoked— Dryden's greatest work began several months after the Dorset Garden production of *The Kind Keeper*. In September, 1678, Titus Oates, a one-time student of the Jesuits, later turned Protestant zealot, legally deposed before Justice Edmondbury Godfrey details of an extensive Catholic (or "Popish") plot to reclaim England for the Church. When, a month later, Godfrey was found murdered (by whom it is still not known), Oates' allegations of plans for a massacre of Protestants, the assassination of Charles II, and the establishment of the Catholic James as king produced an effect of near hysteria in the London public —a state compounded still further by the exposé of another plan to Catholicize England, discovered in the papers of the Duke of York's secretary, Father Coleman. The extreme Protestant Whigs in Parliament, led by the Earl of Shaftesbury and the Duke of Buckingham, siezed upon this evidence as a means of opposing the succession of the Catholic James and of advancing the claims of Charles' illegitimate son, the Protestant Duke of Monmouth. Charles and his Tory supporters, who feared the danger of abridging the constitutional principle of hereditary succession far more than the threat of Catholic subversion, repeatedly withstood Parliamentary attempts to pass a bill which would "exclude" James from the succession. The last of these attempts—which Charles convened at Oxford to avoid the Whiggish faction in the city and which he promptly dissolved after a week on March 21, 1681—marked the defeat of the Opposition: and in July, Shaftesbury was imprisoned in the tower to await trial later in the year.

It is impossible that Dryden could have remained uninvolved in these events. Since the Restoration, he had been a champion of Charles and an advocate of monarchy; and, as Historiographer Royal, he was an official propagandist for the present government. Temperamentally sceptical, he would have regarded the sort of commitment which results in political faction as a form of dogmatism; and, if these reasons were insufficient for his entry into the political arena, he found both his old enemy, Buckingham, and a new enemy, Thomas Shadwell, united in the Opposition against the king. In the epilogue to what may have been his most recent work since Oates' original testimony, *Troilus and Cressida* (1679), Dryden's satirical references to the politics of the day begin, and they continue in the dedication of *The Kind Keeper*, published late in the same year; in passages of the dialogue of *The Spanish Friar* (1680); and in other prologues and epilogues written at the time. It is possible, too, that he may have entered the pamphlet war waged during the Whig's efforts to pass the Exclusion Bill; at least one anonymous tract of the time is attributed to him, *His Majesty's Declaration*

Defended (1681), a defense of Charles' own published justification of his dissolution of Parliament. With the lapsing of his salary from the theater and the delays in the payment of his pension, Dryden was probably now in real financial distress, and, if the writing of political propaganda were materially rewarded, we may suppose that he would not decline other opportunities to express what were, after all, his deepest convictions.

Shaftesbury's trial in November, 1681, offered another opportunity of this sort. Dryden's response was *Absalom and Achitophel*, a satirical poem written to prejudice the town and, if possible, to induce the jury to return a "True Bill": a verdict finding Shaftesbury guilty of treason. Published anonymously about two weeks before the trial, the work provoked a storm of Whig attacks upon Dryden, who was no doubt quickly identified as the only poet capable of the poem. But although *Absalom and Achitophel* was a personal success for Dryden, it failed in its political purpose. A grand jury, handpicked by Whig sheriffs, threw out the bill of indictment to the immense satisfaction of Shaftesbury's adherents, who struck off a medal to commemorate their victory. Encouraged, perhaps, by Charles himself,[31] Dryden produced early in 1682 his own memorial of the occasion, *The Medall*, a satirical exposure of the madness of London's behavior. This work, too, was answered by the Whigs, two of whom—the dramatists Thomas Shadwell and Elkanah Settle—Dryden immortalized as epitomes of the intellectual poverty and the literary ineptitude which he found in the attacks of all his opponents. They appear, respectively, as Og and Doeg, along with the satiric portraits of a half-dozen other Whig worthies which Dryden contributed to Nahum Tate's sequel to *Absalom and Achitophel*, published late in 1682. Shadwell, who had in the same year distinguished himself from his colleague by satirizing Dryden in *The Medal of John Bayes,* was repaid with triple measure by the unauthorized publication in the same year of *Mac Flecknoe*, a mock-heroic tribute to "T. S." as the incarnation of Dullness and, early in the next year, by some remarks in the "Vindication of the Duke of Guise," Dryden's answer to Whig criticisms of the party play by that name which he had written with Nathaniel Lee.

Shortly after the Restoration, Dryden had begun—and then had abandoned—a play which dealt with the apparent parallel between the plot of the Holy League against Henry IV of France and that of the Covenanters against Charles I. In 1682, Dryden saw the actions of the Protestant Opposition to Charles II as an even closer parallel to the religiously inspired rebellion of the Guisards. England, he believed, had more to fear from its own sects than from the Catholics, whose alleged plot against the throne had become for the Whigs a means of attaining their own political ends; "Plots, true or false," he had written in *Absalom and Achitophel*, "are necessary things, /To raise up Common-wealths, and ruin Kings" (11. 83-84). Papal infallibility, to be sure, assumed the right to "Depose and give away the Right of any Sovereign Prince"; but still more dangerous, since no Penal Laws controlled them, was the assumed "Infallibility" of the private spirit of the Protestant fanatics which authorized the same "Doctrines of King-killing and Deposing"; ". . . the most frontless Flatterers of the Pope's Authority," Dryden wrote in the preface to *Religio Laici*, "have been espous'd, defended, and are still maintain'd by the whole Body of Nonconformists and Republicans. 'Tis but dubbing themselves the People of God, which 'tis the interest of their Preachers to tell them they are, and their own interest to believe; and after that, they cannot dip into the Bible, but one Text or another will turn up for their purpose. . . ."[32]

In view of this intimacy of religion and politics, it is not surprising that Dryden should, in 1682, have focused his thoughts upon the question of authority in scriptural interpretation. From the viewpoint of that natural scepticism to which he had more than once admitted, the recent civil disturbances provided the most compelling evidence yet of the need of a higher authority than human reason or the private spirit, both of which, he believed, were motivated by private interest. Such an authority he defines in *Religio Laici*, an essentially fideistic confession of his own faith in terms of the minimal credentials of scriptural revelation (i.e., those articles of faith which, though unverifiable, are nevertheless believed as absolutely necessary for salvation). Sceptically opposed to both Deistic and Sectarian dogmatism, yet unable to disregard the political implications of papal infallibility, Dryden identified his personal religious beliefs with the broad *via media* of Anglicanism. But his orthodoxy seems more expedient than genuine, for the strongly antirational emphasis of this poem cannot have stopped short of Anglicanism and the latitude of opinion which its moderation encouraged. As *The Duke of Guise* and the preface to *Religio Laici* indicate, Dryden in 1682 still regarded the political aims of the Catholic Church as inimical to English interests; but *Religio Laici* provides ample evidence of his temperamental readiness to submit to an omniscient authority in spiritual matters.

Although by the beginning of 1683 the greatest threats to the continuance of a Stuart on the English throne had passed, Dryden's work as a Tory propagandist continued throughout the remaining years of Charles' life and on to the end of James' brief reign. Two of the works produced in the next two years were commissioned by the king: the translation of the Calvinist historian Louis Maimbourg's authoritative *History of the [French] League* (1684), and the libretto of an opera, *Albion and Albanius* (1685), by the French composer Lewis Grabu, celebrating the history of the House of Stuart. Dryden was probably paid for his work on both projects, but certainly not sufficiently to relieve those "extreame wants, even to arresting," which he mentions in a plea for money to Charles' treasurer, Laurence Hyde.[33]

It was no doubt by necessity, then, that he embarked on a series of commercial ventures with Jacob Tonson, the enterprising publisher he had joined after leaving the King's Company. In 1679 Dryden had contributed a preface and three translations to an edition of Ovid's *Epistles* which Tonson was compiling from the work of several translators. A similar but more ambitious project was under way in 1683—a translation, by some forty men, of *Plutarch's Lives*, for which Dryden wrote the dedication and an introductory biography of the moralist. In the following year appeared the first of Tonson's Miscellanies, *Poems . . . By the Most Eminent Hands*, but chiefly by Dryden, who is represented by his three great satires, by a number of unpublished prologues and epilogues, and by four translations. He apparently found verse translation a congenial as well as a profitable form of writing, for in the second volume of the Miscellanies, entitled *Sylvae* (1685), his contribution included renderings of a good part of Lucretius and of four Horatian odes, along with a preface setting forth his theory of translation, an art that in the years to come was to be his chief form of literary labor.

III *1685-1700*

The death of Charles on February 6, 1685, need not have greatly changed the circumstances of Dryden's career. Since he had, in any work written in behalf of Charles, also looked forward hopefully to the eventual succession of the Catholic James, there is little reason to believe that he regarded his Anglicanism as a cause for discrimination in the new reign. Accordingly, his pensions as Laureate and Historiographer Royal were renewed, along with those of other loyal holders, within the week of James' coronation.[34] Dryden's conversion to Catholicism sometime before the end of 1685 is more likely to be explained then as the logical conclusion of his religious development in the preceding years than as a practical expedient of the moment. In 1682, Dryden's Anglicanism was—if not unorthodox—highly personal in its scepticism of any dogmatic claims to certainty based upon reason. The very existence of the sectarian offshoots of Anglican rationalism testified to the need of an omniscient authority, one, however, which Dryden's own undogmatic fideism could not supply. There is, moreover, a point at which scepticism itself becomes dogmatic, "a kind of positiveness in granting nothing to be more likely on one part than on another," he wrote in 1684, in the "Life of Plutarch."[35] It was apparently in this light that Dryden, in 1687, regarded the sceptical faith of *Religio Laici*; the choice of what was and what was not necessary to be believed had been his own; and merely resolving not to impose it upon another did not guarantee its certainty. "To take up half on trust, and half to try"—what he had earlier considered "an honest *Layman's Liberty*"—he now regarded "but bungling Biggottry."

That Dryden's conversion was not, as his enemies maintained, an act of opportunism is also indicated by his complete commitment to the Catholic cause at a time when the immoderation of James' actions would have made silence the wiser policy. In 1685 he wrote *A Defence of the Papers written by the Late King . . . and Duchess of York* ("Papers" in which Charles confessed to having been reconciled to the Catholic Church); and, in 1688, the year in which James arrested seven Anglican bishops for refusing to read from their pulpits the Declaration of Indulgence granting immunity to the Catholics, Dryden translated Dominique Bouhour's *Life of St. Francis Xavier.* But the clearest evidence of his sincerity is found in *The Hind and the Panther* (1687), a formal apology of Catholicism and of his own break with the Anglican Church, written with full knowledge of the brevity of Catholic supremacy in England. In June of 1688, Dryden celebrated, in *Britannia Rediviva,* "the birth of the Prince," an event which, by threatening to extend the reign of Catholicism, hastened its collapse. Six months later the Protestant William and Mary mounted the throne which James was forced to vacate, and in March of 1689 Dryden's old enemy Thomas Shadwell became the new Poet Laureate.

There is at first a temptation to sentimentalize the account of the remaining eleven years of the poet's life. At fifty-eight, Dryden's most substantial fortune was still the Northamptonshire lands he had inherited years before from his father; and, as a member of a hated religion in the now alien England of William and Mary, there was no hope that the future would change this condition. "Against his will," as he wrote in the preface to the tragedy *Don Sebastian* (1689), he returned "to dig . . . [the] exhausted Mines" of the theater, a fate which was no doubt doubly unpleasant when his efforts were not greatly welcomed by the public. *Don Sebastian* was "insupportably too long" to have met with more than a cool reception; his next play, *Amphitryon* (1690), was a spirited farce based upon Plautus and Molière, but both it and the opera *King Arthur,* which appeared the following spring, had a musical accompaniment by Henry Purcell to recommend them to the public. And, referring to the delays to which *Cleomenes,* a tragedy produced in 1692, was subjected, he remarked that "had it not been on consideration of the Actors, who were to suffer on my account, I should not have been at all sollicitous, whether it were play'd or no."[36] Not unexpectedly, in view of these facts, he announced his retirement from the theater in the prologue of his next play, the tragicomedy *Love Triumphant* (pub. 1694).

The note of disappointment in Dryden's remarks about the theater at this time is not, however, to be attributed to Protestant prejudice of the playwright: he simply appears once and for all to have wearied of the uninformed criticism to which the drama by its very public nature was subject; and in the prologue to *Don Sebastian,* he wittily agreed to accept his punishment as a Catholic if he might enjoy his freedom as a dramatist. It is, in fact, surprising that Dryden was not subjected to greater prejudice from the many political enemies he had made in the former reign. Fortunately he had still some friends in high places—his brother-in-law Sir Robert Howard, Charles Sackville, to whom he had dedicated the *Essay of Dramatic Poesy,* and others. These men, we may expect, not only protected him from much persecution; they were also the source of such charity as he acknowledges of Dorset in the *Discourse concerning . . . Satire.* Indeed, now that he was freed from the constant distractions of public affairs, he may have found the more relaxed pace of his life rather pleasant. He found time to enjoy the lionizing attention of the younger writers who patronized Will's coffee house and to study his favorites of the past, the translating of which now became his chief occupation. He frequently visited his own Northamptonshire lands or the estates of friends, where he was able to indulge his love of country pleasures—one of which, we learn with some surprise, was fishing.

But it was in his work—his translating—that Dryden found, if not comfort, then the greatest satisfaction and also the most lucrative source of income in his later years. He turned as to old friends to Persius and Juvenal (1692); to Ovid (whose *Metamorphoses* appear in *Examen Poeticum* (1693), a fourth volume of Miscellanies); to Virgil, and to Chaucer and Boccaccio, He more than once speaks in the prefaces written at this time of having been caught up and mastered by his authors. The translation of Virgil, to be sure, entailed more than three years of arduous and unremitting labor (1693-97) and a return to his earlier life of working under the pressure of deadlines and of the cares of financial considerations (for the edition was published by subscription). But the great investment of time and the steady drain upon his health was not regretted, and in the end, he felt the project "more happily perform'd than I could have promis'd my self."[37] Not more than a year passed before he undertook another volume of translations for Tonson, *The Fables;* and, though the varied nature of its contents (narratives chiefly by Ovid, Chaucer, and Boccaccio) was less demanding than his previous work, his constant battle against illness throughout most of 1699 probably made the work no less taxing upon his powers. Two months after the appearance of *The Fables*, he died on May 1, 1700, presumably of an attack of erysipelas.[38] Only a few weeks before, however, he had finished a "Secular Masque," written for a performance of Fletcher's *The Pilgrim*, revived by his friends in the theater as a benefit for the dying poet. The "Masque" is an allegorical summary of the age of James I, the Civil Wars, and the reigns of Charles II and James II (symbolized by Diana, Mars, and Venus), the age of which Dryden was so much a part. One wonders if its final lines, a warmly human perspective of the past and the future, had not a special significance for their author:

> Momus.   All, all of a piece throughout;
> Pointing
> to *Diana*.   Thy Chase had a Beast in View;
> to *Mars*.   Thy Wars brought nothing about;
> to *Venus*. Thy Lovers were all untrue.
>   *Janus*. 'Tis well an Old Age is out,
> Chro[nos]. And time to begin a New.

CHAPTER 2

Literary Background and Early Poems

Although Dryden published nothing in the nine years following
the appearance of his two earliest poetic efforts—the elegy
"Upon the Death of the Lord Hastings" (1649) and the commendatory verses to John Hoddesdon (1650)—it is likely that he
was employed in the practice of his craft during this period,
for in his next productions, the "Heroique Stanzas" to the
memory of Cromwell (1659) and *Astraea Redux* (1660), his
talent for adjusting the rhythms and cadences of verse to the
requirements of meaning is already apparent. Here, for example,
are some couplets from the latter poem:

> For his long absence Church and State did groan;
> Madness the Pulpit, Faction seiz'd the Throne:
> Experienc'd Age in deep despair was lost
> To see the Rebel thrive, the Loyal crost:
> Youth that with Joys had unacquainted been
> Envy'd gray Hairs that once good days had seen:
> We thought our Sires, not with their own content,
> Had ere we came to age our Portion spent.[1]

There is little promise of such mastery in the elegy on Hastings,
where, for example, Dryden consoled the young lord's "*Virgin-
Widow*" in these lines:

> O wed
> His Soul, though not his Body, to thy Bed:
> . . . .
> Transcribe th' Original in new Copies; give
> *Hastings* o' th' better part: so shall he live
> In 's Nobler Half; and the great Grandsire be
> Of an Heroick Divine Progenie. (11. 97-104)

Conforming to the prosodic practice of his age, the young
Dryden punctiliously counted his syllables (the sole exception
occurring in the extra syllable of "th' Orig(i)nal"), and in
doing so he resorted to ugly elisions at three places in the

lines. But clearly, and also typical of the time, Dryden's paramount concern is the sense of the passage, with the result—
as often in Donne's satires, though without his rewarding com-
pensations—that the limitations of the couplet are working
against his meaning rather than with it as in the passage
from *Astraea Redux*. We might, in passing, notice how, by
failing to exploit the potential of couplet rhetoric, these lines
lack the point and effectiveness achieved in the later poem
by antithetical construction. There, the caesura of the second
line brings *madness* and *pulpit* into contrast with *faction* and
throne; the caesura of the fourth line sets the *thriving rebel*
against the *crossed loyalist;* and the closure of the second
couplet sets *age* against *youth*. The lines from Hastings' elegy
also bring together antithetical elements—*soul* and *body, the
original* and *new copies,* and *the better part* and *nobler half;*
but they fail as antitheses because Dryden had not yet discovered
the advantage of rhyme and of the medial caesura to punctuate
the sense of the couplet.

Not only in versification, but in rhetoric too, the Hastings
elegy was typical of its time. Dryden's lines are filled with
specimens of Metaphysical wit in the debased form in which
Cowley and Cleveland passed on that tradition at midcentury,
a form which perpetuated the fondness for intellectual play
with philosophical abstraction expressed in shockingly concrete
imagery, without, however, the emotional impulse which, in
Donne's conceits, lifts the imagination to great heights. We
have already observed that the prosodic lapses of the "Elegy"
are due to the intellectual weight which the lines are forced
to carry; we may now notice that Dryden was concerned there
with the development of a conceit based upon the discernment
of similarities and differences between the marriages of *souls*
and *bodies*. It must be remembered that Hastings' death by
smallpox on the eve of his wedding would have been regarded
as not only a personal tragedy but also as a national tragedy
since it obstructed the joining of two powerful noble families.
Dryden therefore conceived of a wedding of souls through
Hastings' death as a more ideal union than the wedding of
bodies—purer and, for the state, more noble and enduring—
for it would propagate only the best and eternal qualities of
the father, "th' *Idea's* of his Vertue, Knowledge, Worth . . .

an Heroick Divine Progenie" (11. 100, 104), qualities which, it is suggested, might serve as the panacea of the sinful nation and the foolish noble youth of the time. "Erect no *Mausolaeums*," he decorously concludes in the final extension of the conceit, "for his best/Monument is his Spouses Marble brest."

As formal consolation, this conceit is not entirely out of keeping with the better features of Dryden's early work. It is impossible, however, to be as charitable with other examples in the elegy: the elaborate analogy of Hastings' moral and intellectual virtues in learned astronomical terms (11. 27-42); the likening of the smallpox blisters to a foil (which sets off the young man's beauty) and to "Rose-buds, stuck i' th' Lily-skin about" (11. 56-58); and this, perhaps the grossest absurdity of all:

> Each little Pimple had a Tear in it,
> To wail the fault its rising did commit:
> Who, Rebel-like, with their own Lord at strife,
> Thus made an Insurrection 'gainst his Life. (11. 59-62)

But even this figure is no worse than some others by more mature contributors to the volume commemorating Hastings' death. As Ruth Wallerstein has pointed out, such witty ingenuities with the causes of death had been recommended by rhetoricians as formal "motives" of elegiac composition.[2] Moreover, Dryden's example, with its references to "Rebel" and "Insurrection," contributes to the level of social significance which has been noticed in the final lines of the poem. Nevertheless, although Dryden never ceased entirely to employ the conceit, he soon learnd to avoid such extravagancies. By 1668 he used the pejorative term "Clevelandism" to describe such strained attempts at wit: in the *Essay of Dramatic Poesy*, Engenius remarks that "we cannot read a verse of Cleveland's without making a face at it, as if every word were a pill to swallow: he gives us many times a hard nut to break our teeth, without a kernal for our pains."[3]

I *The Literary Background*

We have dwelled this long on an obviously inferior poem in order to indicate the sort of ground out of which the young poet grew and to provide a mark by which we can gauge his development in the years before his paramount concern in writing was the theater. Much of what we shall have to say about Dryden's evolving conception of wit and poetry must wait upon the specifically critical pronouncements of his prose prefaces; but four years before the first of these, in a slight commendatory poem prefixed to Sir Robert Howard's 1660 publication of *Poems*, Dryden expressed some views on poetry which already indicate the lines along which we have suggested his development would take place. His poetics here were based upon the opposition of natural genius—what Addison would later call "the mere Strength of natural Parts . . . without any Assistance of Art or Learning"[4]—and the poetic spirit which submits itself to the control of art. The products of the first are characterized by strength and wildness, those of the second by sweetness and smoothness; and Dryden begins by saying that there is a music "uninform'd by Art . . . which shames Composure [composition], and its Art excells" (11. 1-6). Art itself is cold; its regularity can dampen the warmth of all but a "strong Genius." Yet beauty in poetry is not the "child of Chance"; Dryden would not "dare . . . such a doctrine here admit,/As would destroy the providence of wit" (11. 33-34). If even the birds, which are "better taught at home, yet please us lesse," then the natural genius of the poet requires the control and restraints of art. Without these, metaphors which, with "dangerous boldnesse," soar to heavenly heights, inevitably fall and betray when they do so their origin in the "sand and dirt" of this world (11. 11-14). But, although art is required to idealize the natural materials of poetry, that art is best, Dryden says, which conceals itself. In fact, beauty in poetry is the ideal combination of both strength and sweetness, the whole made to appear natural.

Dryden's lines to Howard do not merely repudiate the examples of midcentury practice which we have observed in his elegy to Hastings: they indicate a conception of the function of art and of the role of Nature in art which is fundamentally different from that which produced his first work. As Louis Bredvold has explained, the Aristotelian view of art as an idealized imitation of nature tended during the seventeenth century "to approximate the Platonic vision of a beauty which exists above and beyond the actual world and of which the actual world partakes only imperfectly."[5] Syllabic regularity, for example, had little if any effect upon the sense of the elegy to Hastings; in the lines to Howard, however, Dryden indicates (in terms of Denham's famous comparison of the movement of verse to the Thames River) that the function of versification is to improve or idealize the matter of poetry, "as when mighty Rivers gently creep,/Their even calmnesse does suppose them deep" (11. 9-10). Similarly, the wit of the Hastings elegy is the product of "genius" which is uncontrolled by art. But in the lines to Howard, Dryden speaks of the "providence of wit," a way of knowing that is both mysterious—all-knowing, but untaught—and also, in its identification with "Care" rather than with "Chance," an acquired discipline. In 1660, then, Dryden conceived of wit as a balancing of "genius" and "art," or, in the terms in which he expressed it in his first critical preface, of "imagination" and judgement."

The view of poetry which we are suggesting that Dryden took in 1660, a view which may in general be termed Neo-classical in the role it assigned to reason or judgment as a control of the imagination, constituted a critical phase in what W. K. Wimsatt has called the "long struggle . . . between the custodians of pure idea and pure fact, dialecticians and scientists, on the one hand, and on the other, the custodians of the riches of the 'word,' grammarians, rhetoricians, critics, exegetes."[6] It will be remembered that Socrates, as a representative of the former group, caused the rhapsode Ion to admit that poetic utterance is a form of divine madness which does not tell us anything that is, scientifically speaking, true. In the centuries preceding the Renaissance, however, scientific truth was not always opposed to rhetoric, the close ally of poetry; and the ability to think wisely was not always divorced from the ability to speak gracefully. Witness the fact that among the five established parts of Rhetoric, as taught in the Trivium, or traditional grade school curriculum, the intellectual activities of "invention" and "disposition" (the discovery and arrangement of materials) were shared by both Rhetoric and Dialectic or logic. In the middle of the sixteenth century, however, the French logician Peter Ramus again caused the separation of the faculties of thinking and speaking by making invention and disposition parts of Dialectic alone, leaving to Rhetoric only elocution, or style, and delivery.[7] One of the results of this redistribution was a type of poetry which, in order to be taken seriously, cultivated a manner adhering to the rigorous honesty and plainness of scientific writing and employed the artifices of style as mere external ornamentation to make the instruction palatable.

Supporting this academic hostility to the resources of poetry were the severe criteria of truth advanced by Cartesian philosophy and the strong inducements toward plainness in literary style recommended by post-Baconian science. The principle of the French philosopher René Descartes that truth was that alone which could be clearly conceived restricted what could actually be considered knowable to abstractions which were only the mathematical properties of things, and it ignored as truth the nonverifiable properties of things on which poetry as well as religion traditionally depended. "The Cartesian spirit," Basil Willey has said, "made for the sharper separation of the spheres of prose and poetry": "the cleavage then began to appear . . . between 'values' and 'facts'; between what you *felt* as a human being or as a poet, and what you *thought* as a man of sense, judgment and enlightenment."[8]

In this situation the poet had either to make his writing as conformable to the laws of reason as he could, or lightly to pass it off as patent make-believe. Nor was his function simplified by the directives on the scientific use of language arrived at by the Royal Society. Bishop Thomas Sprat, who published its *History* in 1667, recorded that the members had resolved "to return back to the primitive purity, and shortness, when *men* deliver'd so many *things,* almost in equal number of *words.* They have exacted from all their members, a close, naked, natural way of speaking: positive expressions; clear sense; a native easiness: bringing all things as near the Mathematical plainess, as they can."[9] Even a poem as Metaphysical in imagery as Dryden's elegy on Lord Hastings nevertheless reflected the dialectical shift which was taking place in the emphasis and the method particularly of religious discussion during the years between Donne and Dryden. "Religious argument," according to Ruth Wallerstein, "had ceased to concentrate on the mysteries and on the contempt of the world and had focused on the affirmation of the rational nature of the soul of man."[10] Thus Dryden's elegy employs the "essay type of development" appropriate to rational discussion; and, although it combines the traditional forms of the Classical lament and of the older theological elegy, Dryden adapted its elements to a pattern of rational thought, stressing, as we have noticed, social rather than religious implications in his handling of the conventional considerations of immortality and Providence.

The converse of an attitude which places its trust in demonstrable, universally verifiable knowledge is a suspicion of knowledge which is personal and private. To the rationalist of the seventeenth and eighteenth centuries, the poet who claimed to be poetically inspired was to be taken no more seriously than the religious enthusiast who claimed to be religiously inspired. Even Dryden's early commendatory verses to John Hoddesdon "on his divine Epigrams" may with good-natured irony have alluded to this association of poetic and religious inspiration. Referring perhaps to his young friend's fondness for paradox and pun in poetry, as well as to the fact that his poems consisted of divine epigrams, Dryden remarked, "What may we hope, if thou go'st on thus fast!/Scriptures at first; Enthusiasmes at last!" (11. 17-18).

In the seventeenth century—and particularly after the emotional indulgences of the Civil War—imagination came to feel the restrictions that were placed upon religious enthusiasm, with which, as a highly peculiar and therefore untrue mode of perception, it was identified.[11] Thus wit—a way of knowing which was identified, until the first half of the century, with the ability of the imagination to discover resemblances in vastly different things—came to be opposed to judgment, the faculty of reason to discover differences between generally similar things. Dryden's statement in *Religio Laici* that "a Man is to be cheated into Passion, but to be reason'd into Truth," expresses this view; but this was written in 1682 at a time when he was earnestly endeavoring to state the truth of his religious convictions. His expression of heroic themes in the poems we shall examine now, however, constitutes a halfway point between the extremes of imagination and judgment that is consistent with the meaning of his phrase the "providence of wit."

II *The Restoration Poems*

In all, Dryden published ten poems by 1667. Occasional rather than "pure" poems, they range from the panegyrics on the Protector, Charles II, and the city of London to complimentary epistles addressed to personal friends or to influential personages whose friendship was worth cultivating. The first of these, the "Heroique Stanzas Consecrated to the Glorious Memory of . . . Cromwell," was published in 1659, just one year before the first of his celebrations of the return of Charles II and the monarchy to England. As we have noted in Chapter I, Dryden's enemies later seized upon this apparently rapid conversion to substantiate their charge that the poet was a turncoat; but Samuel Johnson's apology should satisfy the most exacting critic on this point: if Dryden changed, he said, he changed with the nation.

One wonders, moreover, how great a change it really was for Dryden. The tribute to Cromwell carefully avoided discussion of party principles and refrained from complimenting the Protector's successor, a panegyric to whom, as Scott observed, "was a natural topic of consolation after mourning over the loss of his father."[12] Dryden conceived of Oliver's actions as having been called forth by historical circumstances to which, by virtue of his natural greatness, he was equal. Far from suggesting approval of the execution of Charles I (as Thomas Shadwell attempted to interpret it), Dryden's statement that Oliver endeavored "to stanch the [nation's] blood by breathing of the vein" (1. 48), refers only to the war, which we are hereby to understand was a painful, but necessary evil. Ten years earlier, he had attributed Hastings' death (the withdrawing of Heaven's "Pledge") to the "Nations sin," and had expressed his horror of regicide in the smallpox-rebel analogy—an unnatural violation of beauty and order. As a man of his age, Dryden responded to the return of monarchy in much the way that he responded to the current tendency to subvert the "wanton wits" of the first half of the century: in both the political and the aesthetic realms, the change implied the overthrow of the instabilities of unassisted human nature and a return to an authority and order which is conformable to the laws of reason and nature.

This change he openly acknowledged in his verses to Sir Robert Howard, whose "successful Pen"

> Restores the Exil'd to her Crown again;
> And gives us hope, that having seen the days
> When nothing flourish'd but Fanatique Bays,
> All will at length in this opinion rest,
> "A sober Prince's Government is best." (11. 50-54)

But Dryden's verses to Cromwell are their own apology. Following the models of Waller and Sprat (his co-authors in the volume in which his poem was first published), he chose as his genre the formal panegyric in alternately rhyming quatrains, a verse form which had become associated with the heroic poem through William Davenant's use of it in *Gondibert* (1651), and which Dryden, in 1667, considered "more noble, and of greater dignity, both for sound and number, than any other verse in use amongst us."[13] Accordingly, Cromwell appears to us as a national hero, as one whose greatness Dryden could measure in terms not of his own admiration of the man but of that man's contributions to England as witnessed by the entire world. Whatever Dryden's personal opinion of Cromwell and of the political philosophy for which he stood, his intention "to draw a *Fame*" is rightly understood as both "our duty and our interest too," and its impartial justness is apparent in the concessions to Cromwell's "Heroique Vertue" which even his political enemies were forced to make.[14] So conceived, Cromwell appears as a personified force, definable on the one hand in terms of such abstractions as "Grandeur," "Vertue," and "Fortune" and with such conventional symbols as *"Palmes," "Laurells,"* and *"starrs,"* and on the other by a catalog of his domestic and foreign accomplishments. Character is slighted since it is relative to historical circumstance, Providence, or "Fortune." Like Heaven's original, which "shew'd a Workman's hand . . . perfect yet without a shade" (11. 59-60), Dryden's portrait of Cromwell is emblematic—it might have been struck off on a medal, as might also the equally abstract portraits of Charles in the poems which followed it. But the latter are primarily celebrations of a historical event, the significance of which, in view of the richer emotional texture of the poems, touched Dryden more deeply than the accomplishments of any individual.

From the crest of enthusiasm to which the nation rose in 1660, Dryden conceived of the return of the rule of monarchy as the advent of a golden age of peace and security after the oppressive, martial iron age of the Commonwealth. The "Heroique Stanzas" had already celebrated Cromwell as a war-like peacemaker, the final lines even incorporating that conventional symbol of peace traditionally associated with the political calm of the reign of the early Stuarts: "And *Warrs* have that respect for reprose,/As *Winds for Halcyons* when they breed at Sea" (ll. 143-44).

But political chaos returned with the accession and rapid collapse of Richard Cromwell, and although *Astraea Redux* begins by noting a cessation of hostilities, the "Peace" which describes the conditions of England in its opening lines is unnatural and unreal, "a dreadful Quiet . . . worser farre/Then Armes, a sullen Intervall of Warre" (ll. 3-4). It was a peace enforced not by law and justice, but by arbitrary power; and, as Dryden develops this idea by contrast first with the peace of Sweden and then with the concord which existed between France and Spain, we see that it is far more symptomatic of disorder, sickness, and unhappiness in the state than of their opposites. (At his death, the contentious Charles X of Sweden appointed regents to follow a policy of pacification for his "now guideless Kingdom," and by the marriage of Louis XIV and the Infanta Maria Theresa, "the fair *Iberian* Bride," France and Spain appeared miraculously reconciled.) Real peace, Dryden seems to be saying, is a perpetuity of peace, depending upon a succession of experienced leaders whose strength proceeds from the authority of established law and right. Hence the English envy of the concord between France and Spain, actualized by the assurance of its continuity under an established succession of monarchy: "We sigh'd to hear the fair *Iberian* Bride/Must grow a Lilie to the Lilies side" (ll. 17-18).

The poem, then, celebrates an expanded conception of peace, and Dryden employs the notions of wise and experienced *guides* in government, of youthful vitality and procreativity (suggested by various forms of the marital imagery just noted), and, as we shall see, of the hopes of atonement and the forgiveness of former guilt to serve throughout the poem as the index of national well-being. Thus, the plight of England is expressed in a figure of marital estrangement ("Our cross Stars deny'd us *Charles* his Bed/Whom Our first Flames and Virgin Love did wed" (11. 19-20), and by a reference to the fearful paralysis of the peerage, the "Scarlet Gown" of whose authority (in the absence of the monarch) aroused not the pride, but the rage of the vulgar, as a red flag does a bull, or in Dryden's words, "like sanguine Dye to Elephants": "Nor could our Nobles hope their bold Attempt/Who ruin'd Crowns would Coronets exempt" (11. 29-30).

Similarly, the identification of the rebellious "Vulgar" and "their designing Leaders" with the Classical antitypes of civilization—the lawless one-eyed Cyclops blinded by Ulysses, and the monstrous son of Earth, Typhoeus, who "violated" Jove and Heaven—suggests not only the ideas of barbaric fury and presumptuous rebellion, but also the specific causes of England's malaise as conceived in the poem: the overthrow of wise leadership by blind zeal, and the degrading of joyful union by the violence of lust and rapine ("Their blood to action by the Prize was warm'd" (1. 34). England's internal enemies have inverted national values (the "Rebel" thrives, the "Loyal" is crossed); poisoned them at their sources, the Church and Throne (occupied now by "Madness" and "Faction"); and emasculated the real sources of national strength: "Experienc'd" Age and Youth. The former now "in deep despair was lost," while "Youth that with Joys had unacquainted been/Envy'd gray hairs that once good days had seen" (11. 25-26).

Only the return of a monarch—which according to Charles' Declaration of Breda meant the "restoration both of king, and peers, and people, to their just, ancient, and fundamental rights"[15]—only the return of a Charles can deliver England from its plight and grant to the nation the complete and perpetual "Peace" that the first forty-nine lines of the poem describe. Those who have criticized *Astraea Redux* for political inconsistency, for extravagance of praise, or for religious impropriety must admit that Dryden's espousal of Charles is at least warranted in the context of the poem, however unjustified it may be outside of that context. England's woes were the king's woes, "who thus/Was forc'd to suffer for Himself and us" (11. 49-50); and Dryden's tribute to Charles is based upon the potentially tragic idea that in suffering man learns: "How

shall I then my doubtful thoughts express," he asks, "that must
his suff'rings both regret and bless" (11. 71-72). Charles' exile
was a "Pilgrimage" that developed courage, patience, political
wisdom, and skill:

> Well might the Ancient Poets then confer
> On Night the honour'd name of *Counseller,*
> Since struck with rayes of prosp'rous fortune blind
> We light alone in dark afflictions find. (11. 93-96)

But of even greater importance than these virtues—which, after
all, Dryden attached to Cromwell in the "Heroique Stanzas"—
was the guarantee of justice inherent in the concept of the
king as a legal head of the government, to which Dryden draws
our attention in the reference to Astraea in the title and in the
epigraph of the poem.

The myth of Astraea came down to the poets of the sixteenth
and seventeenth centuries in the lines of Virgil's Fourth Eclogue,
written also in a troubled time of civil war, but predicting a
new age of peace and security under the aegis of Augustus
Caesar. It tells of the return, after her flight from the Earth
in the Iron Age, of Astraea, the virgin goddess of Justice, an
event which, according to Virgil, would usher in a second Golden
Age of Saturn:

> The last age told by Cumae's seer is come,
> A mighty roll of generations new
> Is now arising. Justice now returns
> And Saturn's realm, and from high heaven descends
> A worthier race of men. Only do thou
> Smile, chaste Lucina, on the infant boy,
> With whom the iron age will pass away.
> The golden age in all the earth be born.[16]

In view of the traditional association of Astraea with imperial
and secular power during the reign of Elizabeth, it is natural,
as H. T. Swedenberg, Jr., has said, that Dryden should have
employed the myth to connote "the return of law and of kingly
power," and have turned "the Virgilian prophecy into a compliment to Charles".[17]

> Oh Happy Age! Oh times like these alone
> By Fate reserv'd for Great *Augustus* Throne!
> When the joint growth of Armes and Arts forshew
> The World a Monarch, and that Monarch *You.* (11. 320-23)

But England's joy at the Restoration depended as much upon Charles' Act of Oblivion, which was to forgive his enemies, as it did upon the Declaration of Breda; and in at least one seventeenth-century adaptation of the myth of Astraea, Dryden could have found the return of Justice associated with the return to the earth of Charity and Mercy. Centuries of Messianic interpretation had made Virgil's eclogue a prophecy of the birth of Christ and of His salvation of men. Milton thus incorporated it, together with Psalm lxxxv, in the *Ode on the Morning of Christ's Nativity;* along with Justice, according to Milton, came "meek-eyed Peace," Truth, and Mercy, "thron'd in Celestial sheen." Christ's ultimate significance as man's Redeemer is thus telescoped in the advent of Christ's peace by an allusion to the traditional "Four Daughters of God" who allegorically argue the conflicting claims of justice and mercy in God's mind.[18] For Dryden, the perfect peace which England has been denied depended upon a similar reconciliation of opposing principles.

The nation need not, the poem is saying, fear Charles as the personification of uncompromising Truth and Justice; for, as the "Prince of Peace," he is also the embodiment of mercy:

> A voice before his entry did proclaim
> *Long-Suff'ring, Goodness, Mercy* in his Name.
> Your Pow'r to Justice doth submit your Cause,
> Your Goodness only is above the Laws. (11. 264-67)

Hence the resumption, in the second half of the poem, of the earlier marital imagery, coupled at times with frequent allusions to Christian history. The rift between the nation and her royal groom is seen as a trivial lover's quarrel "when once they find their Jealousies were vain," and now "with double heat renew their fires again" (11. 213-14). With the symbolic change of the name of the ship, *Naseby* to the *Charles,* the long-delayed marriage is formally consummated. Dryden treats this miraculous reconciliation, "a gift unhop'd without the price of war" (1. 140), as a new Covenant of Grace—as a blessing freely given by Heaven which "we could not pay for," but for which Christlike Charles offered himself as the redeeming sacrifice. Accordingly, the effect upon the nation of Charles' *coming* (like Astraea's, a return, but a springtime return) is developed in terms which suggest both the promise of the

Nativity and the assurance of the Resurrection. In his exile, Charles was "forc'd to suffer for Himself and us"; the delays and premature royalist attempts to restore Charles ironically echo the scriptural anticipations of Christ's arrest and ultimate delivery from suffering ("Th' Attempt was fair; but Heav'ns prefixed hour/Not come" (11. 147-48); the reappearance of Charles' birthstar, overcast by clouds at his "Morn," outshines the "Suns meridian light" and guides "our eyes to find and worship you" (1. 291). Then, the nation is assured, "tears of joy for your [Charles'] returning spilt,/Work out and expiate our former guilt" (11. 274-75).

Astraea Redux ends, then, on the promise of England's salvation through the peaceful reconciliation of justice and mercy. The three poems which followed it—the coronation panegyric *To His Sacred Majesty* (1661), the New-Year's Day gift to Edward Clarendon, Charles' Lord Chancellor (1662), and the epistle to Dr. Charleton (1663),—express the fulfillment of that promise. *To His Sacred Majesty* conveys the sense of the nation's complete satisfaction in its love of the king (Dryden's subtle rendering of the subdued spirit of the anticlimactic coronation), of the "full fruition" of its joys which ascend to Charles in his now unqualified divinity, as the anthems of the celestial choir ascend to God. The marital imagery of *Astraea Redux* reappears in the references to Charles as Commander of the "Mistress of the Seas," as *pater patriae,* and, in the passage referring to his choice of a bride, as father-to-be: "Choose only," his subjects pray, "that so they may possesse/With their own peace their Childrens happinesse" (11. 135-36). The nation's faith in the advent of a new age, suggested in this poem by images of spring and by the reference to the receding waters of the Deluge, is related to the New Year's Day occasion of the lines to Clarendon, and the poem also appropriately stresses the "active" waging of peace through the administration of justice. In view of his role as mentor to the exiled Charles and as Lord Chancellor—the "Chanel" of "vital influence" dispensed by "the Nations soul (our Monarch)"—it is not surprising to find Clarendon's fate closely associated with the king's. But here Dryden's references to the Restoration are as relevant to Clarendon's earlier efforts as a poet as they are to his achievements as a politician. Clarendon, by helping to restore Charles, also helped to restore the muses:

> When our Great Monarch into Exile went
> Wit and Religion suffer'd banishment
>
> . . . .
>
> At length the Muses stand restor'd again
>
> . . . .
>
> And their lov'd Druyds seem reviv'd by Fate
> While you dispence the Laws and guide the State. (11. 17-26)

In this poem, as in the earlier lines to Robert Howard, allusions to the Restoration constitute what has been called "a basic ordonnance that gives shape and meaning to other matters"[19]— to poetry and to the practical administration of justice; and in his next, the epistle to Dr. Charleton, to science, and to an archeological treatise on the origin of Stonehenge. The epistle to Charleton is a compliment prefixed to Charleton's published theory that the ancient ruin was a Danish coronation palace and not, as Inigo Jones argued, a Roman temple. As Earl Wasserman has demonstrated, Dryden handled Charleton's treatise as a "radical image" that could assimilate the values associated with the work of other English scientists, and thereby function analogically with the political facts of the Stuart regime "to show that all things testify to the glory of the crown."[20] The poem thus permits us to say that Charleton's thesis is validated by virtue of Charles' restoration; for, as both the anointed ruler by ultimate descent from God and as the elected ruler by the people, the king does in poetic fact make what was before the Restoration considered a "Temple" *become* a "Throne": "His *Refuge* then was for a *Temple* shown:/But, *He* Restor'd, 'tis now become a Throne" (11. 57-58).

The epistles to Clarendon and Charleton and the earlier lines to Sir Robert Howard make Dryden's acceptance of royalist principles appear to have been indeed a wholehearted commitment, touching his way of thinking about not only politics, but poetry, science, and apparently human affairs in general. In these poems, Dryden's conception of English monarchy has become an "all-pervading providence in the human realm that, operating simultaneously at all levels, makes one explicate and validate another."[21]

Annus Mirabilis (1667), the poet's tribute to London's loyalty and courage during the Year of Wonders, 1666, offers still another and perhaps more daring instance of this sort of poetic exploitation of the Restoration; for Dryden *used* in this poem, the idea of the Restoration as a means of reinterpreting as national triumphs a series of events which a malcontented minority were construing as the acts of God's displeasure at England's acceptance of monarchy. Already in 1661 and 1662, three pamphlets, all of them distinguished by the words *Mirabilis Annus* in their titles, recorded instances of natural "prodigies" to this effect;[22] and the jeopardy of national security in 1666 by the threat of economic depression through commercial rivalry with Holland, by the renewed outbreak of the plague, and by the great fire which destroyed half of London might easily have constituted for the credulous even stronger testimony of England's waywardness at the Restoration. Dryden, who attributed the truncation of Hastings' dynasty to the "Nations sin," was not himself beyond attaching a supernatural cause to natural happenings; but his strategy in *Annus Mirabilis* was perforce more subtle, since he could not, by merely inverting the interpretation of the omens, make himself liable to the presumption of which royalists accused the republican prophets.[23] Instead, his description of the fire as a *Walpurgisnacht* revel of the "Ghosts of Traitors" and "bold Fanatick Spectres" (stanza 223) clearly links the fire to the recent uprising of Fifth-monarchy men and perhaps to the crime of insurrection in general, as do also the stanzas which describe the growth of the conflagration in terms of a rebellion:

> Such was the rise of this prodigious fire,
>   Which in mean buildings first obscurely bred,
> From thence did soon to open streets aspire,
>   And straight to Palaces and Temples spread. (11. 857-60)

But the "Wonders" to which Dryden's title refers are not the prodigies of the year conceived of as signs of God's judgment; they refer to the "true Loyalty, invincible Courage and unshaken Constancy" of the citizens of London in the face of such trials: "To submit your selves with that humility to the Judgments of Heaven, and at the same time to raise your selves with that vigour above all humane Enemies . . . I know not whether," he wrote in the dedication of the poem, "such trials have been ever parallel'd in any Nation . . ." (I, 42-43). So interpreted, the events of the year gave cause for praising the city, not for blaming the king; for Dryden they served to consolidate and test the strength of the people under trial: "Providence has cast upon you want of Trade, that you might appear bountiful to your Country's necessities; and the rest of your afflictions are not more the effects of God's displeasure . . . then occasions for the manifesting of your Christian and Civil virtues" (I, 43).

Moreover, to the extent that these afflictions were no less the king's than the nation's the poem shows—in Charles' personal attention to the outfitting of the fleet, in the wisdom with which he came to the aid of the ruined city, and in his un-selfish prayer for its deliverance—the reciprocity of bounty and of "Christian and Civil virtues" between king and subject. As the now familiar marital imagery of the dedication of the poem suggests, the events of the year tested that union which was enthusiastically anticipated in *Astraea Redux* and formally ratified in *To His Sacred Majesty*: "You have come together a pair of matchless Lovers, through many difficulties; He, through a long Exile, various traverses of Fortune, and the inter-position of many Rivals, who violently ravish'd and with-held You from Him: And certainly you have had your share in sufferings" (I, 43).

This echo of the theme of the Restoration poems is signifi-cantly developed throughout *Annus Mirabilis*. As Charles' exile had earlier been conceived of as a means of inculcating strength and wisdom, so the sufferings of the people in the fire, the plague, and the war are now viewed as the means by which they have been strengthened in the wisdom of unity and loyalty; as Charles had been associated with the great themes of redemption and rebirth, so Dryden describes the city as "a great emblem of the suffering Deity"; and as Charles had accomplished, in his kingly power and his embodiment of law and ancient rights, the restoration of the nation to peace and security in 1660, so the people, in their united strength and loyalty, accomplished its restoration in 1666. "One part of my Poem," Dryden concluded in his dedication to the city, "has not been more an History of your destruction, then the other a Prophecy of your restoration" (I, 43).

Annus Mirabilis is thus both an historical poem and a

panegyric. As a historical poem it undertakes to chronicle the naval victory of the English over the Dutch and the progress of the fire. These events, together with the men involved in them, are heroic; yet Dryden says the poem is not, properly speaking, an epic. For one thing, its detailed inclusiveness ties it "too severely to the Laws of History"; for another, the action is not single but double. Dryden's theme is the *reciprocity* of friendship and goodness that existed in a time of crisis between the people and their king. The narration of the naval battle celebrates the ability of the people to "sustain a nations fate" through "passive aptness," a form of heroic virtue in which private destiny is merged with national destiny, not without advantage at last to the individual: "The doubled charge his Subjects love supplies,/Who, in that bounty, to themselves are kind" (ll. 181-82).

Significantly, the narration of London's trials begins with an apology for the error of all "who in the night of Fate must blindly steer" (l. 140), and this passage is followed by two examples of loyalty unwisely placed: the alliance between Holland and France, whose "weak assistance will his friends destroy" (l. 160); and that between England and the Bishop of Munster, who taught "the *English* first/That fraud and avarice in the Church could reign" (ll. 147-48)—a warning, no doubt, to those who were likely to align themselves with the religiously motivated opposition. But the loyal efforts of the English in the war are reciprocated by Charles, who, during the fire, fits his royalty to "the levell'd use of humane kind" (l. 664). He lacks neither the "pow'r" (l. 959), nor, as "God's Annointed," the means (l. 1144) to sustain his subjects.

As the narrator of a panegyric, Dryden allowed himself the epic poet's liberty "to express his thoughts with all the graces of elocution, to write more figuratively, and to confess, as well the labour as the force of his imagination" (I, 47). His "graces of elocution" include the use of unnaturalized Latin idiom; a wide variety of imagery borrowed from Virgil, his acknowledged "Master in this Poem"; and the heroic stanza. His imaginative "labour" may be seen in the transformation of the historical victories of the year into the more miraculous victory of the people of London over their own doubts and weaknesses, a victory which, in its guarantee of loyalty tested in suffering, and in its promise of a glorious future for the nation, is described in the imagery of redemption and salvation that had earlier been used to convey the significance of Charles' restoration. Dryden describes the fleet sent on the *third* day of battle to reenforce the vessels commanded by Albemarle as the "new *Messiah's* coming" (1. 454); and, in the original version of stanza 105, he associates it with the resurrection (there is "something divine" in a fleet which "dead and buried the third day arose").[24] The recently commissioned warship, *London,* built and outfitted at the city's expense, and a symbol therefore of "Loyal London," is associated, in the reference to the "*Phoenix,*" with the idea of rebirth and renewal—as is also the final significance of the burning of the city:

> More great then humane, now, and more *August,*
> New deifi'd she from her fires does rise:
> Her widening streets on new foundations trust,
> And, opening, into larger parts she flies. (11. 1177-80)

The poet's note on the first of these lines reminds us that *Augusta* was "the old name of *London";* as the name of the emperor who brought peace and security to Rome, it had also become popularly attached to Charles, and was so applied by Dryden in *Astraea Redux.* In thus identifying London and the king by a common name as well as by a common effort, Dryden expresses, in the belief that the people and the king are united in the national interest, the heroic ideal which in the years to follow informed first his tragic drama and later his satire.

CHAPTER 3

Essays on Dramatic and Heroic Poetry

The prose Preface to *Annus Mirabilis* was signed from Charl͵ ton, Wiltshire, where Dryden and his wife had moved som͛ time in the summer of 1665 to escape the infection of the plague. While there he also wrote an Essay of Dramatic Poesy, which used the English naval victory over the Dutch on June 3, 1665, as the context for a vindication of "the honour of our English writers, from the censure of those who unjustly prefer the French before them."[1] Modern research has revealed that one of "those" to whom Dryden was referring was the Frenchman Samuel Sorbière, whose *Relation d'un Voyage en Angleterre* (Paris, 1664) included among other things some uncomplimentary remarks on English theater.[2] The *Essay* was thus important as a reply to Sorbière, and as such it constituted "an international engagement [comparable] at another level" to that being fought at sea by the English and the Dutch.[3] But Dryden also spoke of it "as an amusement to me in the country," written "without the help of books, or advice of friends" (I, 27): "Seeing then our theatres shut up [because of the plague] I was engaged in these kind of thoughts with the same delight with which men think upon their absent mistresses" (I, 23).

In addition to its historical occasion, then, the *Essay* is of interest to us as a record of Dryden's private reflections on questions about the nature of drama, questions which were to concern him throughout his career, and as a dispassionate essaying of the conflicting answers to these questions offered not only by the French and English but by the critics of all ages. Dryden later described this method of inquiry as "sceptical" (i.e., as unwilling to claim as a certainty any of the arguments considered): "That it is so, not only the name will show, which is *an Essay*, but the frame and composition of the work. You see it is a dialogue sustained by persons of several opinions, all of them left doubtful, to be determined by the readers in general" (I, 124). As we shall see, Dryden had something more than an objective interest in the views of one of these speakers. Neander (an anagram for *Dryden,* and a denomination for the "new-man," coined from the Greek *neo* and *andros?*)[4] not only fulfills the author's intention of vindicating the English against the French dramatists, but also states his defense of the use of rhyme in drama (published a year earlier in the dedicatory epistle to *The Rival Ladies*) and attempts, as Dryden does in much of his dramatic criticism, to combine foreign and native elements in a unified concept of Neoclassical drama. For reasons which will soon be clear, we shall for the present, however, regard the four speakers of the *Essay* as representatives of the more or less distinct views of drama which Dryden himself might have shared and, at best, as only partial portraits of the historical personages identified by tradition.[5]

I Neoclassical Imitation and The Essay of Dramatic Poesy

Different as their arguments are, the four speakers of the *Essay* are united by their common acceptance of the "description" of a play (and of the general nature and end of all narrative) according to Classical principles: ". . . a play ought to be *A just and lively image of human nature, representing its passions and humours, and the changes of fortune to which it is subject, for the delight and instruction of mankind*" (I. 36).

We may notice three critical topics here: first, the source of poetry, the Classical conception of "nature" (or specifically "human nature," characters and actions); second, the means of poetry, Aristotle's *mimesis,* imitation, or representation; and third, the function of poetry, Horace's pleasure-profit formula (*utile dulce*), the instruction and delight of the reader. In no sense did the Classical concept of the imitation of "nature" mean a literal copying of the "great outdoors." "Nature," for the ancients, was the general and unchanging order which was perpetually operating in the universe. In imitating this order, the poet produced images of the essential and persisting *forms* of things, ignoring their temporal, local, or accidental aspects. If, for example, a king were to be imitated in a play, Dryden believed that "in all his actions and speeches, that person must discover majesty, magnanimity, and jealousy of power" (I, 214), even though the model of one's own ruler happened to embody the very opposite qualities in his personality. Accordingly, it was believed that "Nature always intends a consummate beauty in her productions, yet through the inequality of the matter the forms are altered . . . For which reason, the artful painter and the sculptor, imitating the Divine Maker, form to themselves, as well as they are able, a model of superior beauties" (II, 118). Dryden's translation here from the Italian Neoplatonist Bellori expresses the idealistic bias of his source: the represented image of "nature" in art is superior to the unreal shadows of ideas in the world of matter.

But without denying the reality of our world of phenomena, Aristotle had said much the same thing: ". . . Poetry is something more philosophic and of graver import than history, since its statements are of the nature rather of universals, whereas those of history are singulars. By a universal statement I mean one as to what such or such a kind of man will probably or necessarily say or do . . .[6] Thus by ignoring the irrelevancies of history or biography and by rearranging things in a necessary or probable order, the poet, according to Aristotle, represents *"the way things would be if the form, the principle, that is operating through them were carried out to its logical fulfillment, its final completion."* [7]

Given, then, the universal order of nature as his source, the poet must strive to exemplify its forms in the medium of words, to make of them—in the terms of Lisideius' "description" of a play—"a just and lively image." If the forms imitated by a poet are rendered faithfully (i.e., if their outlines are fully represented and their various elements duly ordered according to the principles of probability and necessity), then their images will be both internally consistent ("just") and lifelike ("lively"). The insistence here upon both qualities is significant, for it insures that a play is not an abstract statement but a concrete image. Philosophy may instruct us of the truths of nature, but it will not *delight* us. By stating things as they should be in concrete terms, by exhibiting "truth" in images which can move us, literature became for the ancients an adjunct of moral education.

It was the labor of succeeding centuries to "methodize" or to codify these Classical conceptions of art into a system of rules; the tradition extends from Horace, through the sixteenth-century treatises on poetics by the Italians Vida and Castelvetro and the Frenchman Julius Scaliger, to the seventeenth-century restatement by Corneille, and then to its most rigorous English exponent Thomas Rymer. As originally conceived, the Neoclassical rules of art aimed at achieving decorum and symmetry in imitation and at maintaining probability through the handling of parts as they contribute to a whole. Horace, for example, ruled that Medea should not butcher her children on the stage, nor Atreus cook human flesh in public because such *unnatural* acts would leave the audience incredulous. "If the rules be well considered," Dryden later quoted Rapin as saying, "we shall find them to be made only to reduce Nature into a method, to trace her step by step, and not to suffer the least mark of her to escape us: 'tis only by these, that probability in fiction is maintained, which is the soul of poetry. They are founded upon good sense, and sound reason, rather than on authority" (I, 228). But even though the rightness of the rules could be theoretically justified by their relation to nature and the laws of reason, their practical influence upon many critics was authoritarian; for they tended to divert the attention of writers *from* "nature," and to limit imitation either by the precedent of those ancients from whom the rules derived, or by the common sense criteria of an approximate realism. Nature and Homer were the same: so ran the first article of the Neoclassicist's faith. As Aristotle had noticed, many of the ancients contrived their dramatic actions singly, without interruption or variation of interest; many of their plays, moreover, limited the time and place of the action to the time of its representation and the space of its stage. By following their example, a play might be justified as an imitation of nature: thus was the most characteristic regulation of Neoclassical criticism—the doctrine of dramatic unities—ratified as a law. Imitation of "nature" had become imitation of Classical models; and probability, "the soul of poetry," had become synonymous with verisimilitude.

In the *Essay of Dramatic Poesy*, the position of extreme dependence upon ancient models is assumed by the first of the speakers in the dialogue, Crites, whose purely doctrinaire attempt to "prove" the superiority of the ancients over the moderns is an all too easy sacrifice to the cool logic of his opponent, Eugenius. Assuming that each age has a peculiar genius for perfecting a particular study, and that full perfection in poetry had been attained by the ancients (as in science it had been attained by the moderns), Crites believes that modern writers may at best expect merely to equal the excellence of the ancients—and then only with "much labour and long study" of their works. But in an age in which poetry is less highly esteemed than science, there are few encouragements and rewards for taking such pains; and the modern poet, "neglecting to look on" the "perfect resemblance" of nature in the works of the ancients, has ventured to render nature himself and has given us "monstrous, and disfigured" representations of her. The most "regular" play, "the nearest imitation of nature," according to Crites, follows the three dramatic unities, which "were delivered to us from the observations which Aristotle made, of those poets, which either lived before him, or were his contemporaries: we have added nothing of our own" (I, 38).

Crites' argument rests on nothing more than an assumption that progress is limited by the "universal genius" of a particular age and on an uncritical faith in the full "maturity" of Greek drama (I, 36). As his adversary Eugenius recognizes, Crites neglects entirely to "prove" that the ancients "wrought more perfect images of human life than the moderns" (I, 44). To resolve the question of superiority in favor of the moderns, then, Eugenius need only turn the first of Crites' assumptions to his own advantage ("if natural causes be more known now than in the time of Aristotle, because more studied, it follows that posey and other arts may, with the same pains, arrive still nearer to perfection"—I, 44), and illustrate the defects of the ancients and the excellencies of the moderns. Of the former, he offers ample evidence: Greek drama, lacking the symmetry of division by acts, did not reach full maturity; not only did it fail to strictly observe the three unities, but one of them (the unity of place) is not even to be found among Aristotle's observations of ancient drama. In thus "swerving from the rules of their own art . . . they have ill satisfied one intention of a play, which was delight" (I, 50); and worse in their "indecorum" (e.g., their ignorance of the concept of poetic justice), they fail even to instruct (I, 50). For Eugenius, the advocate of reason, progress in art is inevitable and necessary; the value of the ancients must therefore be seen in historical perspective:

> we own all the helps we have from them . . . but to these assistances we have joined our own industry; for, had we

sat down with a dull imitation of them, we might then have
lost somewhat of the old perfection, but never acquired
any that was new. We draw not therefore after their lines,
but those of Nature; and having the life before us, besides
the experience of all they knew, it is no wonder if we hit
some airs and features which they have missed. (I, 43-44)

Accordingly, his confidence in the value of the rules depends not
upon their derivation from the works of the ancients but upon
their basis in purely rational principles—the same principles
presumably in which "nature" itself consists. For Eugenius, moreover, rational order is prior to natural order, not coexistent with
it: the ancients, he says, swerved from the rules "by misrepre-
senting Nature to us" (I, 50). Here, conformity to the rules is
conceived of not as the means of imitating "nature," but as an
end in itself, a formal excellence not necessarily related to "nature." Eugenius, for example, criticizes the hackneyed plots
("you see through them all at once") and stereotyped characters
("indeed the imitations of Nature, but so narrow") of the ancients, insisting even that these faults destroy that "one main
end" of drama, delight. Yet, he goes on, "in how strait a compass soever they have bounded their plots and characters, we
will pass it by, if they have . . . perfectly observed those three
Unities . . ." (I, 48).

Eugenius' faith in the efficacy of the rules is thus as uncritical as Crites' trust in the value of the ancients as models. Both
are deductive thinkers, arguing from different major premises,
and Eugenius no more adequately demonstrates the excellencies
of the moderns (the second aim of his argument) than did
Crites those of the ancients. At the end of his speech, Dryden
simply tells us that "Eugenius, who seemed to have the better
of the argument, would urge no farther" (I, 55). Eugenius indeed explodes the myth of the superiority of the ancients; their
imitations, he shows, lack both the requisite liveliness and justness of drama. But in what does the superiority of the moderns
consist? Apparently, since he accounts Neander's "opinion of
our plays . . . the same with mine" (I, 56), it is in the new
"airs and features" which the freer English dramatists have
"hit" in their "excellent scenes of passion." But Eugenius' equal
enthusiasm for the correctness of the moderns would, in practice, abolish such freedom. As W. P. Ker has pointed out, there

were actually two modern arguments against the authority of the ancients, one in the interests of greater freedom for the poets, the other in the interests of the greater correctness of the moderns; "these new Moderns [who employ the second of these arguments] are really more ancient and more pedantic than Gabriel Harvey [a sixteenth-century Crites who tried to enforce Classical meters upon English poetry]."[8] Eugenius' views are thus expressive of the divergent tendencies in Neoclassical criticism after the absolute authority of the ancients had been broken. His is a hypothetical position, one made truly representative only in the arguments for French correctness and English freedom.

Lisideius, the apologist for French drama, therefore begins his discourse by acknowledging his agreement with Eugenius concerning the ancients, but asking further "whether we ought not to submit our stage to the exactness of our next neighbours" (I, 56.). Another reasoner from causes to effects, Lisideius, however, does not assign himself the task of demonstrating the excellencies of French drama—indeed, he mentions not a single French play by name. Assuming, as did his predecessor, that regularity is tantamount to excellence, that instruction and delight necessarily result from imitations which preserve the credibility of an action, he is satisfied to rest his case on French observance of the dramatic unities and the laws of decorum—their insistence on poetic justice and "verisimility," and their narrowing of the range of representative passions and actions to those which, when "imitated to a just height . . . will make a deeper impression of belief in us" (I, 63)—and on the English neglect of these self-evident signs of correctness. For Neander, his antagonist, such thinking mistakes the "rules" as ends in themselves rather than as the means to an end. French drama is indeed more regular than English, he begins, but "those beauties of the French poesy are such as will raise perfection higher where it is, but are not sufficient to give it where it is not" (I, 68). The question being debated, as Neander sees it, is not whether French virtues and English faults (as determined by the "rules") are sufficient "to place them above us," but whether French plays or English plays best fulfill the "description" of a play which all had agreed on at the beginning of the discussion.

To this end, Neander emphasizes those terms of the description

which have been only lightly touched upon or completely ignored by his three predecessors: the *liveliness* of the dramatic image
and its capacity to *delight* the audience. Thus far in the dialogue, these qualities have been conceived of as being contingent
upon the *justness* of the image and its capacity to instruct. For
Neander, however, "the lively imitation of Nature being in the
definition of a play, those which best fulfil that law ought to
be esteemed superior to the others" (I, 68). Not only is the idea
of *justness* subsumed in the world 'lively", but, a few lines later,
Neander implies that an image is only truly "just" when it is
"lively": the beauties of French poetry (which are just in the
sense of being correct) "are indeed the beauties of a statue,
but not of a man, because not animated with the soul of Poesy,
which is imitation of humour and passions" (I, 68). What is
lively has here become not merely what is lifelike in its appearance, but what is lifelike in its effect and arouses our sense of
"concernment" for the characters or "that malicious pleasure . . .
which is testified by laughter." In this way are the instances of
English irregularity justified.

Lisideius argued that the native tragicomedy could not accomplish the ends of drama because it confounded the audience,
"who, before they are warm in their concernments for one part,
are diverted to another; and by that means espouse the interest
of neither" (I, 57). But Neander argues that mirth both increases the effect of concern for tragic characters (as in logic,
"contraries, when placed near, set off each other") and renews
our spirits for still greater concern ("we must refresh it sometimes, as we bait in a journey, that we may go on with greater
ease" [I, 69-70]. All the "quick turns and graces" of plot and
speeches, the qualities of English drama which, if not actually
condemned by Lisideius, are opposed to the formal regularity of
the French, are in this way accounted for: "Grief and passion
are like floods raised in little brooks by a sudden rain; they are
quickly up; and if the concernment be poured unexpectedly in
upon us, it overflows us: but a long sober shower gives them
leisure to run out as they came in, without troubling the ordinary current" (I, 72).

But in defending the rich variety of the English drama, Neander does not believe that he is subverting the Neoclassical values
of decorum and regularity. Not only does he show the advantages

of English freedom in achieving the ends of the "rules," but he devotes much of his discourse to illustrating the observance of those laws in English drama:

> We have many plays of ours as regular as any of theirs, and which, besides, have more variety of plot and characters; and secondly, that in most of the irregular plays of Shakespeare or Fletcher (for Ben Johnson's [sic] are for the most part regular) there is a more masculine fancy and greater spirit in the writing, than there is in any of the French. I could produce, even in Shakespeare's and Fletcher's works, some plays which are almost exactly formed. (I, 78-79)

In appealing here to two standards of excellence, Neander does not, however, arrive at the dilemma we have noticed in Eugenius' argument; the rules, Neander said at the outset, "will raise perfection higher where it is, but are not sufficient to give it where it is not" (I, 68). Native "spirit" and Neoclassical regularity need not then be irreconcilable; we find them combined in a "perfect play" (*The Silent Woman*) by Ben Jonson, whose relation as artist (or "pattern of elaborate writing") to Shakespeare, the natural genius (and "father of our dramatic poets") parallels the relation of Virgil to Homer (I, 82). Before all else, Neander *loves* the "naturally learned" genius from whose "comprehensive soul" the images of nature are drawn "not laboriously, but luckily" (I, 79-80). But, like Eugenius, he believes in the inevitability of progress and the necessity of art. Even the reactionary Crites was forced to concede that, if one of the ancient poets lived in the present age, he would be forced to alter many things: "not that they were not as natural before, but that he might accommodate himself to the age he lived in" (I, 55). For the same reason, we are left to assume, Shakespeare would have written differently in the Restoration. Thus Neander's position in the *Essay* is not a compromise of English freedom in the drama but a defense of the English tradition as the fullest development of the Neoclassical conception of dramatic art.

II *Dryden's Critical Temper*

No reader of the *Essay* will deny—nor could its author, in the interests of objectivity, disguise the fact—either that Neander emerges the victor in this dispute or that his views were shared by Dryden. We arrive at this conclusion, however, not because

Dryden has forced his ideas upon us, or treated unfairly those of Neander's opponents, but because Neander appears to have arrived at his opinions scientifically. His predecessors in the dialogue do little more than draw assertions from authority, but Neander attempts to induce probable causes from observable effects[9]; and the reader, Dryden wrote in his dedication, was "to decide it in favour of which part you shall judge most reasonable" (I, 27).

But in spite of the tentativeness with which he thus states his own opinions, Dryden was accused of critical dogmatism. In 1668, his brother-in-law, Sir Robert Howard, prefaced a play called *The Duke of Lerma* with an attack upon the *Essay* and upon its author as one who "laboured to give strict rules to things that are not mathematical [dramatic poetry being one of them]."[10] Dryden's reply, in "A Defence of an Essay of Dramatic Poesy" (1668), restates many of Neander's views: his insistence upon delight as the chief end of drama (I, 113) and upon its essentially ethical nature (I, 121); the rationale for accepting the unities of time (I, 129) and place (I, 126); and the argument in defense of rhyme in serious plays (earlier advanced in the preface to *The Rival Ladies*), which Neander had restated to Crites in a critical coda of the *Essay*.[11] Of greater interest than these arguments, however, is Dryden's explanation of his critical intention in the *Essay;* for, in defending himself against the charge of "being magisterial," he makes explicit a way of thinking which was to become an outstanding characteristic of much of his ratiocinative writing.

In the "Defence of an Essay," Dryden attempted specifically to defend the validity of a critical view which could comprehend objective principles without being arbitrary and dogmatic. Assuming, as the common ground for both poet and critic, the concept of drama as "the imitation of Nature," Dryden argues that if nature exists to be imitated, it must logically follow that "there is a rule for imitating Nature rightly; otherwise there may be an end, and no means conducing to it" (I, 123). This much, then, is certainty; he has "proceeded by demonstration" to show that there are inherent in nature certain principles for composing and judging poetry. At this point, however, certainty ends: ". . . as our divines, when they have proved a Deity, because there is order, and have inferred that this Deity ought to be worshipped, differ afterwards in the manner of the worship; so, having laid down, that Nature is to be imitated, and that proposition proving the next, that then there are means which conduce to the imitating of Nature, I dare proceed no further positively" (I, 123).

Since we cannot know with demonstrable certainty that the principles we have formulated are correct, we can apply them in composition only tentatively, and in criticism with at best "an inclination to assent to probability."[12] Thus, he explains, he has "only laid down [in the *Essay*] some opinions of the Ancients and Moderns, and of my own, as means which they used, and which I thought probable for the attaining of that end" (I, 123). As his analogy of religious worship and poetic practice indicates, Dryden agreed with Howard that one could not dictate "strict rules to things that are not mathematical"; but this did not prevent him from believing that dramatic poetry was an art, or that its principles could probably assist and control the genius of a poet, and guide the judgment of a critic. Dryden, we have already noted, called the method by which he arrived at such a conclusion "sceptical": ". . . my whole discourse was sceptical, according to that way of reasoning which was used by Socrates, Plato, and all the Academics of old, which Tully and the best of the Ancients followed, and which is imitated by the modest inquisitions of the Royal Society (I, 124.).

In view of the fact that art, for Dryden, implied a rational means to the poet's end, and that criticism consisted of the re-application of those means to existing works of art, it seems unlikely that the term "scepticism" is equivalent here to Pyrrhonism, or the suspension of *all* belief. Rather, as Hoyt Trowbridge has argued, since Dryden's method "saves demonstrative certainty in some fields [e.g., in the knowledge that nature is to be imitated, and in the logical conclusion from this that there must be means to that end], while at the same time justifying probable arguments and tentative or approximate results in others," it might better be termed "probabilism," a practical sort of reasoning deriving ultimately from Aristotle and popularized in contemporary logic texts.[13]

In the decade which followed the publication of the "Defence," Dryden reconsidered the relative merits of English genius and Neoclassical rules in the preface to *An Evening's Love* (1671), in the "Defence" of the epilogue to the second part of *The*

Conquest of Granada (1672), and in the preface to *Troilus and Cressida* (1679). Less general than the *Essay* in their praise of the Elizabethan dramatists, and expressing both sympathy with the views of the ultra-Neoclassicist Thomas Rymer, and a more than tentative commitment to the "rules" of dramatic art, these prefaces have raised serious doubts as to their author's critical consistency. It is to be remembered, however, that Dryden wrote them not as a disinterested observer of critical opinion but as an interested professional, eager to achieve success in the drama. "They, who have best succeeded on the stage," he wrote in the epilogue to the second part of *The Conquest of Granada,* "have still conform'd their genius to their age" (I, 160). Here, as in the *Essay,* "genius" is still the primary requisite of poetry and the delightful instruction of the audience still its "general end" (I, 209); but as a practicing dramatist, Dryden was now forced to reckon with the fact that the demands of the age had changed since the time of Shakespeare and Jonson:

> If *Love* and *Honour* now are higher rais'd,
> 'Tis not the poet, but the age is prais'd
>
> . . . .
>
> Our ladies and our men now speak more wit
> In conversation, than those poets writ.
> Then, one of these is, consequently, true;
> That what this poet writes comes short of you,
> And imitates you ill (which most he fears),
> Or else his writing is not worse than theirs. (I, 160-61)

The age imposed new standards of refinement in language and manners and of accuracy in its images of nature; and the rules, in spite of what detractors like Howard said, were "made only to reduce Nature into method" (I, 228). Yet even Dryden's endorsement of current standards of refinement is qualified by the characteristic insistence upon an animating genius which in the *Essay* had distinguished English from French drama. Thus, in the Preface to *All for Love* (1678), he remarked on the need to respect "the bounds of modesty" in representing manners on the stage, but not, as in French drama, to the exclusion of sense and passion. French manners, Dryden believed, were affected and overly nice—"modesty depraved into a vice" (I, 193): "all their wit is in their ceremony; they want the genius which animates our stage" (I, 194).

With respect to rules, then, there is little in these later pre-faces which is not at least implicit in the *Essay*, and Dryden's advocacy of them is entirely consistent with the progessive views of Eugenius and Neander. His only "ambition," he wrote in the "Defence of the Epilogue," is "that poetry may not go back-ward, when all other arts and sciences are advancing" (I, 163). Similarly, his opinion of the Elizabethan dramatists remained essentially unchanged, and if, in the later prefaces, he seems preoccupied with their defects, it is only by way of distinguish-ing their virtues as the models for his own work.

III *The Proper Wit of Drama and Heroic Poetry*

Dryden's ability to maintain a middle-of-the-road course be-tween the extremes of English dramatic freedom and Neoclassi-cal rule—his insistence upon both natural genius and objective standards of excellence in the practical criticism of the drama—was less easily managed in his discussions of the more theoreti-cal subject of dramatic wit. In part, his instability on this sub-ject is due to the shifting values of the term "wit" itself in the seventeenth century, in part also to Dryden's conception of propriety in wit as a matter relative to literary genre. In general, however, Dryden's use of the term bears out W. K. Wimsatt's contention that because of its "near synonymity" with the term *poetry, wit* "had to move as the implicit concept of good poetry moved,"[14] and that, as we have seen, was in the direction of the refinements prescribed by an age of civility. Although our con-cern here is with wit as a literary product, Dryden also used the term with reference to the faculty *in* the poet, a scholastic distinction—according to the Preface to *Annus Mirabilis* (1667)—between "*Wit written*" and "*Wit writing*." The latter is described as "no other than the faculty of imagination in the writer . . . which searches over all the memory for the species or ideas of those things which it designs to represent" (I, 14). In addition to *finding* "thoughts," "ideas," and images, the poet's imagination also *molds* them "as the judgment represents [them] proper to the subject," and adorns them in "apt, significant, and sounding words" (I, 15). The important point here is that "fancy," the name given to the second of these functions of the imagination, is under the regulation of the faculty of judgment, which arbi-trates on matters of propriety. Reason and judgment, we have already seen, provided the best means of apprehending the order and principles which constituted nature. Fancy, Dryden suggests in the dedication of *The Rival Ladies* (1664), is liable to err; as a way of seeing, it must work in the dark, "moving the sleeping images of things towards the light, there to be distinguished, and then either chosen or rejected by the judgment" (I, 1). It is, moreover, "so wild and lawless, that like an high-ranging spaniel, it must have clogs tied to it, lest it outrun the judgment."

Dryden in fact based his argument for the use of rhyme in drama upon this conception of the imagination, for in imposing the difficulty of rhyme upon himself, the poet's fancy "is ready to cut off all unnecessary expenses," and judgment is permitted to "bring forth the richest and clearest thoughts" (I, 8). Dryden's emphasis of the role of judgment in wit should not, however, be considered a depreciation of the value of imagination. The relation of imagination to judgment, a commonplace in the critical writings of Davenant and Hobbes, parallels, for Dryden, the relation of natural genius to the Neoclassical rules; significantly, Dryden preceded the main discussion of drama in the *Essay of Dramatic Poesy* with a satirical description of two types of false wit, the one consisting entirely in "clownish . . . raillery" and verbal play, the other entirely in judgment, which, as literary "plainness," is affected "to cover his want of imagination" (I, 31-32).

The primary fault in the work of the two poets exemplified in the *Essay* is that, for different reasons, their wit is superficial: on the one hand, we are given satire which, for the celerity and difficulty of its wit, "cannot strike a blow to hurt any"; and, on the other, we are given comedy and tragedy which, for its calmness and easiness, "leaves you in as even a temper as [it] found you" (1, 31). The former style, exhibiting the verbal excess of the preceding age, was no longer sanctioned as wit in Dryden's day; the latter, though it conformed to the corrective tendencies of modern standards of refinement "neither has wit in it, nor seems to have it" (1, 32). For Dryden, "*Wit written* is that which is well defined, the happy result of thought, or product of imagination" (I, 14); or, as he defined it in 1677, "it is a propriety of thoughts and words . . . in other terms, thoughts and words elegantly adapted to the subject" (I, 190). Thus, the proper wit of drama is determined by the demands of probability: "where all that is said is supposed to be the effect of sudden thought," the poet must avoid "a too curious election of words . . . or use of tropes" (I, 15). Shakespeare, Dryden believed, often failed to express his wit "according to the dignity of the subject" (I, 172); his wit, and Jonson's too, was of the old fashion condemned in the *Essay*. Yet in spite of his "carelessness," Shakespeare's plays must also have contained genuine wit, for "when he describes any thing, you more than see it, you feel it too" (I, 80); and since "there is fancy, as well as judgment" in Jonson's comic characters, it is "very certain, that even folly itself, well represented, is wit in a larger signification" (I, 172). To reconcile his love of Shakespeare with the demands of probability in drama, Dryden was forced to surrender his distinction between wit as verbal play and wit as imitation of nature.[15] Critical equivocation was unnecessary, however, in discussions of the proper wit of heroic poetry, for the heroic poem aimed at a "lively and apt description, dressed in such colours of speech, that it sets before your eyes the absent object, as perfectly, and more delightfully than nature" (I, 15).

Perhaps only by a strong intellectual effort are we able to understand the veneration in which earlier ages held the heroic poem. "From the days of Petrarch and Boccaccio to those of Dr. Johnson, and more especially from the sixteenth century onward," W. P. Ker has written, "it was . . . studied and discussed as fully and with as much thought as any of the problems by which the face of the world was changed in those centuries."[16] Dryden's dedication to the heroic ideal extends from his early acknowledgment of discipleship to Virgil in the preface to *Annus Mirabilis* to his translation of the *Aeneid* (1697), in the dedication of which he remarks that a true heroic poem "is undoubtedly the greatest work which the soul of man is capable to perform" (II, 154). Two other prefaces written before 1680 considered the nature of heroic poetry and the problems of adapting it to current fashions of dramatic presentation: the essay "Of Heroic Plays," prefixed to *The Conquest of Granada* in 1672, and "An Apology for Heroic Poetry and Poetic License," prefixed to *The State of Innocence* (1677), Dryden's unproduced operatic rendition of Milton's *Paradise Lost*.

As Basil Willey has suggested, at least a part of the reverence of the heroic poem in the seventeenth century was due to its invulnerability to the withering effects of the new scientific criteria of truth: "though it might make use of fiction," he writes, "though its history might be 'fained,' its object was something as important as Truth itself, namely moral edification."[17] For Dryden, too, the heroic poem was "the most noble . . . and the most instructive way of writing in verse, and withal the highest pattern of human life" (I, 154), and its introduction into the drama in the form of "examples of moral virtue" he recognized as a way of making theater acceptable to Puritan righteousness (I, 149). But his concern with the heroic element in literature is not, in these prefaces, as an apology for heroic poetry on moral grounds, but ultimately an apology for all poetry on its own grounds of naturalness and truth as he understood these terms. In the "Defence of an Essay," Dryden said that the naturalness and truth of poetry are not demonstrable, but that the mere preference of "good verse" to "prose" is an adequate argument of its value:

> for if all the enemies of verse will confess as much, I
> shall not need to prove that it is natural. I am satisfied
> if it cause delight . . . for poesy only instructs as it
> delights. 'Tis true, that to imitate well is a poet's
> work; but to affect the soul, and excite the passions,
> and, above all, to move admiration (which is the delight
> of serious plays), a bare imitation will not serve. (I, 113)

The aims of the "serious" dramatist here described are to an even greater degree those of the author of a heroic poem or play. Indeed, if a reader is to be moved by "the highest pattern of human life"—by the persons, actions, and passions of heroic poetry—an even greater effort to "heighten" the imitation of nature is required. Theatrical effects and extravagant flights of fancy which the restrictions of dramatic probability would prohibit "are no more than necessary [in the heroic play] . . . to raise the imagination of the audience, and to persuade them, for the time, that what they behold on the theatre is really performed" (I, 154-55). More respectable than the Elizabethan drama, heroic poetry thus offered Dryden firmer ground for an argument justifying poetic freedom and the license, if need be, to enlarge the bounds of the Neoclassical rules of art.

In the conclusion to "An Apology for Heroic Poetry and Poetic License," Dryden defined wit as "a propriety of thoughts and words" (I, 190); hence, he argued, "all reasonable men will conclude it necessary, that sublime subjects ought to be adorned with the sublimest, and consequently often with the most figurative expressions" (I, 190). The same degree of heightening was required in the heroic play, which "ought to be an imitation, in little, of an heroic poem"—even though the laws governing the latter "indulged him [the author] a further liberty of fancy, and of drawing all things as far above the ordinary proportion of the stage, as that is beyond the common words and actions of human life" (I, 151). But although the heroic play was a special case, Dryden seized upon its sanction of poetic license as a general principle to differentiate poetry from prose:

> This, as to what regards the thought or imagination of a poet, consists in fiction: but then those thoughts must be expressed; and here arise two other branches of it; for if this license be included in a single word, it admits of tropes; if in a sentence or proposition, of figures; both which are of a much larger extent, and more forcibly to be used in verse than prose. (I, 188-89)

It is important to notice two qualifications of this licence, however. First, it does not sanctify the irrational. Poetry, Dryden said in the "Defence of an Essay," must "*be* ethical," that is, though it "dresses truth, and adorns nature," it "does not alter them" (I, 121). The final sanction of the judicious use of "bold strokes"—of tropes which cause a figure "to stand off to sight," as "heightenings and shadows" function in painting—is the fact that they have been a "delight [to] all ages" and hence "must have been an imitation of Nature" (I, 184). Even "things quite out of nature"—hippocentaurs, chimeras, and ghosts—are justified on rational grounds; religions authorize our belief in what is not seen, for "whatever is, or may be, is not properly unnatural" (I, 154), and if such notions are founded on popular belief, "'tis still an imitation, though of other men's fancies" (I, 187). Secondly, poetic liberties "are to be varied, according to the language and age in which an author writes" (I, 189).

This awareness of his unique position in literary history determined, perhaps as much as any other factor, Dryden's peculiar stance as a critic. Conditioned by the cultural pressures of his own time, yet cognizant of his living relation to the literary traditions of England and Europe, he recognized that although nothing is "lost out of Nature . . . everything is altered" (II, 263), and that, consequently, although the role of criticism consists in the discovery of "a standard of judging well," the judgments it makes must necessarily be provisional. For this reason, Dryden's prefaces probably shed more light upon the mind of their author than upon the literary works they discuss. Historically considered, however, the conception of criticism as a continuing experiment in appreciation had an extremely important consequence, for it led Dryden to popularize the conventional preface of the time as a serviceable tool for everyday literary purposes. His peculiar manner of merely entertaining an idea—the tentative approach to truth which his scepticism permitted—found its natural mode of expression in the dialogue and, especially, in the essay, a form which allowed both the freedom to ramble "never wholly out of the way, nor in it," as he says in the preface to the *Fables* (II, 255), and the intimacy of speaking unauthoritatively to his reader. This quality affected the very fabric of his writing, which no longer withholds its meaning (as does so much seventeenth-century prose) until, at the end of the sentence, its grammatical structure is completed; rather, in the total deference to its content, Dryden's prose strikes one as being largely unpremeditated. As George Saintsbury observed, "Dryden had a great deal to say, and said it in the plain, straightforward fashion which was of all things most likely to be useful for the formation of a workmanlike prose style in English."[18]

CHAPTER 4

Comedy and Tragedy

To succeed in the theater, Dryden wrote in the epilogue to the second part of *The Conquest of Granada*, a playwright must adapt his genius to the demands of his audience. He did not add—though, as his criticism of the Elizabethan dramatists indicates, he no doubt realized—that success so purchased could be short-lived; nothing ages as markedly as fashions which place a premium on contemporaneity. But Dryden's plays seem not only old-fashioned but unreal today. The theater for which he wrote was highly exclusive—in modern parlance a "closed-circuit operation," appealing to only a small portion of the potential playgoing public. In all Restoration London, two licensed public playhouses supplied this minority, and even they were forced by financial difficulties to merge in 1682.[1]

Concentrating their creative energies within these narrow bounds and patronizing—as well as patronized by—a jaded and sophisticated élite, the dramatists of the day developed a spectacular, though none too hardy, product of inbreeding, its vitality manifesting itself in either rank abandon or extravagance, its weakness in a refinement that often betrayed its dissociation from the natural world. The degree to which this peculiar flower thrived during the Restoration was, in no small part, due to Dryden. Between 1663, when his first comedy, *The Wild Gallant*, was produced, and 1680, when political crises and the straitened circumstances of the theater led him with renewed interest to nondramatic verse, he put his hand to twenty-one works for the stage—more by far than any other writer in these years;[2] and Dryden's later statement that only one of these (*All for Love*) was written to please himself[3] (one of the few, by the way, which we still appreciate today), may be understood as an indication of the contemporary success which some if not all of his plays enjoyed.

But Dryden and his peers in the Restoration theater did

not escape the criticism of their contemporaries—no more than, in our own day, they have failed to find apologists. In 1671, the Theater Royal presented George Villiers' *The Rehearsal,* a burlesque of the clichés and excesses of the new rhymed heroic plays—and particularly of those by Dryden, the leading exponent of the variety. More serious were the charges of *"Prophaneness and Irreligion"* which the nonjuror Jeremy Collier published in *A Short View of . . . the English Stage* (1698). Collier's indictment of Restoration comedy as "superlatively scandalous," without so much as the precedent "to which most other ill things may claim a pretence . . . a new world of vice found out and planted with all the industry imaginable,"[4] expressed not only the traditional hostility of the Puritans to the stage, but a majority view of the middle-class citizens who were often the subject of the comic dramatists' ridicule. Although some censure of the comedies on moral grounds has persisted, many of the same plays have been found to embody in an age of moral emancipation such virtues as "a deep curiosity, and a desire to try new ways of living". (" 'Here is life lived upon certain assumptions; see what it becomes'," they seem to Bonamy Dobrée to be saying).[5]

On the other hand, an equally objective critic, L. C. Knights, finds that Restoration comedy lacks "the essential stuff of human experience"—certainly not offensive, but, on the contrary, merely boring.[6] Thus the opening song of Dryden's *Marriage à la Mode* (1671), which Dobrée might cite as an instance of the age's interest in sexual experimentation, is, for Knights, an example of barrenness of "genuine sexual feelings":

> If I have Pleasures for a Friend,
>   And farther love in store,
> What wrong has he whose joys did end,
>   And who cou'd give no more?
> 'Tis a madness that he
> Should be jealous of me,
> Or that I shou'd bar him of another:
> For all we can gain,
> Is to give our selves pain,
> When neither can hinder the other. (I, 195)[7]

Since Dobrée and Knights have each referred to this song as a summary of "the whole idea of Restoration comedy"[8] and since Dryden himself spoke of the play from which it came as "perhaps . . . the best of my Comedies" (III, 191), *Marriage à la Mode* will serve as a convenient base from which to conduct our brief survey of his work in this mode.

I *Comic Love*

Though specifically designated as "comedy" when first published, *Marriage à la Mode, The Tempest* (1667), and *The Spanish Friar* (1680) employ the double action, serio-comic pattern of Fletcherian tragicomedy (a play which "wants deaths, which is enough to make it no tragedy, yet brings some near it which is enough to make it no comedy").[9] Neander, in the *Essay of Dramatic Poesy*, defended the use of this old-fashioned mode on the grounds of English temperament, but Dryden, who frequently confessed his shortcomings in comedy, may also have found the romantic sentiments of these plays and of his avowed tragicomedies—*The Rival Ladies* (1664), *Secret Love* (1667), and *Love Triumphant* (1693)—something more congenial to his own temperament.[10] His use of the term "comedy" is not however unjustified; the opening song of *Marriage à la Mode,* for instance, establishes the predominantly frivolous tone and comic theme of the main plot, the ennui of sexual constancy, and the perils attendant upon the quest of variety. This anti-romantic attitude can be found in every one of Dryden's comic plots, his commitment to it as a motive on every social level having the authority of a natural law. Even the innocent Hippolito, the male counterpart of Shakespeare's Miranda in the revised *Tempest,* finds that his love for the first woman he has ever seen is insufficient when he learns that a second woman resides on the enchanted island; and he sweetly replies to Ferdinand's admonition of constancy—"But, Sir, I find it is against my Nature":

> I must love where I like, and I believe I may like all,
> All that are fair: come! bring me to this Woman,
> For I must have her. (III, 199)

Far more sophisticated, but not much more complex than Hippolito are the comic heroes of *Marriage à la Mode*: Rhodophil, who, in his second year of married life, recognizes only too well the "good qualities" of his wife Doralice, and would be content if he "could put 'em into three or four women";

and Palamede, his friend, who, though promised by a wealthy father to Melantha, regards marriage as an incurable disease that may at best "be patch'd up a little" by the aid of a mistress—"that, indeed, is living upon Cordials; but, as fast as one fails, you must supply it with another" (I, 199). The upshot, of course, is that Rhodophil becomes enamored of Melantha, and Palamede of Doralice, the action developing from the frustrated intrigues and near discoveries of the new sets of lovers. "'Tis a pretty odd kind of game this," says Palamede at a climactic scene in which each couple is surprised by the other:

> . . . each of us plays for double stakes: this is
> just thrust and parry with the same motion; I am to
> get his Wife, and yet to guard my own Mistress. (III, 234)

A concession to the public taste for Spanish intrigue, which Neander believed had enforced an unpleasant sameness upon French drama,[11] the coupling of romantic antagonists was nevertheless for Dryden an indispensable plot device, capable of considerable variation. We find it in his first play, *The Wild Gallant* (1663), where Isabel's schemes to promote Loveby's *amour* with Constance facilitate her own designs on Constance's intended husband, Sir Timorous. It appears, with extravagant complexity, in his next written play, the tragicomic *Rival Ladies,* at the end of which three couples are formed: Gonsalvo and Honoria (who throughout the play has been disguised as a boy named Hippolito), Honoria's brother Manuel and Gonsalvo's sister Angellina (also disguised as the boy Amideo), and Gonsalvo's brother Rodorick and Julia, another sister of Manuel. And we meet it again in *The Tempest* (Ferdinand and Miranda, and Hippolito and Dorinda) and in *The Kind Keeper or Mr. Limberham* (1678), in which the hero Woodall cuckolds both a husband and a "keeper," and in doing so plays a wife and a mistress against each other.[12]

But the success of these comic or "gay" couples depends less upon the mechanical variability of their intrigues than upon the speech of the characters themselves: upon the inclusion of "humour" characters and scenes of repartée by which, Dryden believed, English comedy had been made to excel that of the French.[13] Of the first of these features, Neander's analysis of Ben Jonson's characters in *The Silent Woman* may serve as a definition: ". . . by humour is meant some extravagant habit, passion, or affection [especially manifested in conversation], particular . . . to some one person, by the oddness of which, he is immediately distinguished from the rest of men; which . . . most frequently begets that malicious pleasure in the audience which is testified by laughter."[14] The Jonsonian "humour", self-sufficiently comic quite apart from its social implications,[15] is frequently encountered in Dryden's comedies. The early *Wild Gallant* is filled with such characters: Mr. and Mrs. Bibber—the former addicted to jests, the latter to aphorisms—the bashful Sir Timorous, and the epicure Justice Trice. And they persist in the "fumbling" panderer Aldo of the much later *The Kind Keeper* and in his clerical counterpart, the Falstaffian Dominic of *The Spanish Friar* (1680), whose prototype Dryden called "a miscellany of humours."[16]

More characteristic however, are "humours" which depend for their comic effect upon an implicit social standard—in deviating, through ignorance, ineptness, or prejudice, from the norm of refinement in wit, conversation, and manners. In this manner are the "eloquent" Brainsick of *Limberham;* Mr. Moody, the Elizabethan "man," of *Sir Martin Mar-All* (1667); the foppish servant Benito, in *The Assignation* (1672); and the fashionable ladies—Aurelia, in *An Evening's Love* (1668) and Malantha in *Marriage à la Mode.* The type is well illustrated by Melantha, whose only fault, according to her lover, is an excessive fondness for French. Thus, to her maid's remark that she might have "an honourable Intrigue" with Rhodophil, she replies: "Intrigue, *Philotis!* that's an old phrase; I have laid that word by: *Amour* sounds better. But thou art heir to all my cast words, as thou art to my old Wardrobe. Oh Count *Rhodophil; Ah mon cher!* (II, 207).

The repartée ("close fighting") of witty characters was also authorized by the social mode, for "as it is the very soul of conversation, so it is the greatest grace of Comedy,"[17] Although the gay couples of Shakespeare and of Beaumont and Fletcher may have furnished a model for Dryden, the Restoration "chase of wit, kept up on both sides," derived its "delicacy" from the refinements of Charles's court,[18] and its vivacity from the presence of such a gifted actress as Charles' mistress, Nell Gwyn, who played Florimel in *Secret Love* and Jacintha in *An Even-*

ing's Love. These characters—along with Isabelle, in *The Wild
Gallant* and Doralice in *Marriage à la Mode*—are wits of the
first order, able to hold their own against their male opponents
in the verbal game of love and in the amorous stalemates,
the "provisos" or formal contracts of marital freedom and in-
constancy, in which such a game may terminate. Thus Florimel
and Celadon, in the last act of *Secret Love,* agree to marry only
on condition that either may love another with complete freedom
and without fear of the other's jealousy, with the further
"proviso" that since "the names of Husband and Wife hold forth
nothing but clashing and cloying, and dulness and faintness,"
they "will be married by the more agreeable names of Mistress
and Gallant" (V, 69).

The marriage of Rhodophil and Doralice in *Marriage A-la-
Mode* is a test of such a pact; and at the end of the play, it
rests, as does the impending marriage of Palamede and Melantha,
upon quite other views of the degree of freedom proper in
marriage. Jealousy, that "most delicate sharp sauce to a cloy'd
stomach," has both reinterested each of the rightful partners
in one another and enforced a peace by the threat of reprisal.
Both men reject even the limited liberty of "a blessed community
betwixt us four. . . . Wife and Husband for the standing Dish,
and Mistriss and Gallant for the Desert," agreeing instead to
"make a firm League, not to invade each others propriety,"
with Doralice's further "*Proviso,* That who ever breaks the
League, either by war abroad, or by neglect at home, both
the Women shall revenge themselves, by the help of the other
party" (V, 259).

One may object that marriage on such cold-war terms is
in fact no resolution at all; that the premise on which the
comic action of the play rests (that without fresh stimulus,
marriage is a bore) is dropped not because, after examination,
it is found to be unsatisfactory, but simply to bring the action
to a close after the comic value of its premise has been exhausted.
It should be noted, however, that the comic action of many
of Dryden's plays is in fact an examination of the premises
upon which it is based and that, although marriage may appear
in some of them as an expedient, it is at the same time the
lesser of two evils. A life dominated by the caprice of un-
restrained natural passion is as unfulfilled in the domestic state

as it is destructive in the social state; and it is, therefore, not insignificant that the pact in which Rhodophil and Palamede join parodies the social covenant. Marriage with Mrs. Pleasance, after his endlessly frustrated *amours* with Mrs. Tricksy and Mrs. Brainsick, cannot fail to be a satisfying condition for the un-disciplined Woodall of *The Kind Keeper;* and the Mock-Astrol-oger Bellamy, in *An Evening's Love,* has at least one moment's misgivings about the future comforts of an aging roué: "I find constancy, and once a night come naturally upon a man towards thirty," he tells his man Maskall; "only we set a face on't; and call our selves unconstant for our reputation" (III, 274).

Moreover, in the best of Dryden's comedies, marriage is in the end conceived of not merely as the least troublesome means of satisfying physical appetite but as something attractive in itself. Dryden's philanderers and flirts are not so much emotionally as intellectually bored; or, better, they are seeking persons in whom emotional energies and intelligence are naturally united in a lively and refreshing perceptiveness of the world around them. The jealousies of Rhodophil and Pala-mede are aroused not by the suspicion that their rightful partners are secretly exciting as mistresses, but by the discovery that they are wits: "*Palamede* has wit, and if he loves you, there's something more in ye than I have found," says Rhodophil to Doralice—"some rich Mine, for ought I know, that I have not yet discover'd" (V, 258-59). The wit of Dryden's heroes and heroines is not merely the mechanical manipulation of antitheses to which Knights objects; his lovers have the capacity of interest-ing us in themselves, and when they succeed they laugh morality "back into its rightful place, as the scheme which ultimately makes life most comfortable."[19]

II *Heroic Love*

With the exception of the farces (*The Wild Gallant, Sir Martin Mar-All,* and *The Kind Keeper*), the action of Dryden's anti-romantic comic plots is laid on the fringes of courts in Spain, Sicily, and Italy—locations which accomodate the turbulent politics and passions of the serious plots of the tragicomedies.[20] In the latter and especially in the heroic tragedies, love is no longer an idle pastime in which persons may indulge at will; it is a power so overmastering that it inevitably leads its subjects into conflict with earthly and heavenly obligations, either to secure its object or, once obtained, to keep it. Beyond this, it is difficult to generalize about the nature of the love which is so central a part of these plays. "Unquestionably," a recent commentator on the subject has said, "Dryden's heroic love does reflect the sentimental, metaphysical Platonism" of both the French heroic romances, which in many instances furnished his plots, and the pre-Commonwealth Platonic court drama.[21] To the extent, however, that Dryden's heroic lovers are "slaves to their emotions and self-centered ambitions," this Platonic reading has frequently to be qualified by the recognition of Dryden's debt to Hobbesian materialism.[22] In an attempt to comprehend both of these views, Scott C. Osborn has argued that Dryden's heroic plots portray two kinds of love. One is an irrational disease, a "passion caused by a distemper of the bodily humors," which serves as the motivation of the main movement of the play; the other, Platonic love, ideal, spiritual, and wholly consistent with reason, which controls the outcome of the play.[23]

The basic conflict in Dryden's heroic drama, Osborn maintains, is "between passion (as irrational *heroical* love) and reason"; by the end of the play, the "heroical" lover must be either supplanted or rationally *cured* by a Platonic lover.[24] Abdalla's love for the ambitious villainess Lyndaraxa, in *The Conquest of Granada* (1670-71), illustrates this conception of "heroical" love. Purely sensual ("I felt," he says, "the pleasure glide through every part"), this affection immediately overthrows not only his rational duty of loyalty to his brother the king, but, he continues in the analysis of his feelings,

> For such another pleasure, did he live,
> I could my Father of a Crown deprive.
> What did I say!
> Father! that impious thought has shock'd my mind:
> How bold our Passions are, and yet how blind. (Pt. 1, II, 43)

His honor "not wholly put to flight;/But would, if seconded, renue the flight," Abdalla appeals to Zulema for rational counsel "to fortify the better cause"; but the latter, who wishes to avenge a family wrong upon the king, only further weakens Abdalla's resistance to the passion by arguing that "Reason's a staff for age, when Nature's gone;/But Youth is strong enough to walk alone." In the next act, the noble Abdelmelech supplies the needed counsel; another slave to Lyndaraxa's wiles, he offers himself as an example, and argues that reason need not be ruled by the senses:

> . . . our Reason was not vainly lent;
> Nor is a slave but by its own consent.
> If Reason on his Subjects Triumph wait,
> An easie King deserves no better Fate. (Pt. 1, III, 47)

But the advice comes too late, and Abdalla seals his own fate: "I'le love; be blind, be cousen'd till I dye" (Pt. 2, III, 48).

Although many of Dryden's characters manifest the symptoms of this sort of "heroical" love, their actions seldom contribute to a conflict which controls the movement of the play. In *Tyrannic Love*, for example, Porphyrius is willing to "let Honour, Faith, and Vertue flye" (IV, 374) for the sake of his love of Berenice; yet his passion is subordinated to the demands of her virtue—not at the end of the play cured but *throughout* the play kept amenable to her reason. Almanzor, in *The Conquest of Granada*, is an even more striking instance of self-control. "Free as Nature first made man," "humorous as wind," and unsophisticated in the ways of both politics and love, this freedom-loving primitive considers his passion for the noble Almahide a form of slavery. Yet it is the very "excess of love" which enables him to act in accord with reason, as when, because of her betrothal to the king, he relinquishes his own right to her in consideration of her honor. He explains to Zulema, another of Almahide's suitors:

> Had I not lov'd her, and had set her free,
> That, Sir, had been my generosity:
> But tis exalted passion when I show
> I dare be wretched not to make her so. (Pt. 1, III, 57)

Dryden points up the ideal nature of Almanzor's love by immediately contrasting this passage with the opposing demands of Zulema: "If you will free your part of her you may," he tells Almanzor:

> But, Sir, I love not your Romantique way.
> Dream on, enjoy her Soul, and set that free;
> I'me pleas'd her person should be left for me. (Pt. 1, III, 58)

Although Almanzor and Zulema are both subjects of Almahide's beauty, the former is able to suffer physical separation from her. In so doing, Almanzor enjoys a freedom that is denied to Zulema, whose sensual enslavement demands possession of her "person." "Love various minds does variously inspire," says Placidius in *Tyrannic Love*, (II, 351)—and it will appear in the following discussion of his three greatest heroic creations that Dryden did not aim to depict an established conception of love—or of honor. He disapproved of the French habit of showing, at the expense of dramatic interest, what men "were obliged to do by the strict rules of moral virtue." Rather, his heroic plays are experiments in dramatic interest, and to that end they attempt to show "what men of great spirits would certainly do when they were provoked."[25]

III The Conquest of Granada

The dramatic portrait of Almanzor in *The Conquest of Granada* requires the extended canvas of ten acts—two plays in fact; but, unlike the earlier *Indian Emperor* (1665) which contrived to pick up the threads of *The Indian Queen* (1664), the two plays comprising *The Conquest* were two plays obviously conceived at the same time and produced within a month of each other in 1670-71. Moreover, although the two earlier plays foreshadow, in the character of Montezuma and in the cultural setting of Spanish-Christian conquest, the character of Almanzor and Ferdinand and Isabella's conquest of Moorish Granada, these similarities are to be accounted for by the conventions of heroic tragedy—the model for which was the epic—and, in the case of the resemblances of the heroes, by their common origin in Artaban, the hero of La Calprenède's long romance *Cléopâtre* (1647-56). Like their common prototype, Montezuma and Almanzor are of obscure birth (the former was bred in a cave, the latter in the African desert); their origins remain a mystery until, at the end of the plays, their noble parents are revealed. Both, then, in a literal sense are noble savages, and, in view of their influence upon the Mexican and Spanish populaces, heroes of near mythical proportion. Both men are also unsophisticated, guided by feelings rather than logic and, therefore, at a disadvantage among the intrigants of civilized society.

But in "the true romantic sense," the term "noble savage"

is more applicable to Montezuma than to Almanzor, who may be described as a "noble barbarian" or foreigner.[26] In the prefatory note explaining the connection between *The Indian Queen* and *The Indian Emperor*, Dryden says that his aim was to show "the Native simplicity and ignorance of the *Indians*, in relation to *European* Customes" (I, 273), and in *The Indian Queen*, where Montezuma's wildness is apparent even in a civilization whose "customs are by nature wrought," we are led to account for his rash acts of love and valor in terms of a childhood spent among forest beasts:

> . . . th' unlick'd whelp I pluck'd from the rough Bear,
> And made the Ounce and Tyger give me way,
> While from their hungry jaws I snatch'd the Prey. (V, 243)

Both man and society are more highly evolved in *The Conquest of Granada*: Almanzor is a natural man, but not a wild man; and Granada—as the Spaniard Cortez of *The Indian Emperor* had said—is a civilization in which men "by Art . . . unteach what Nature taught" (I, 277). Unlike Montezuma, Almanzor is not intellectually underdeveloped or incapable of adjusting to the ways of civilization. The account of the bullfight at the beginning of *The Conquest of Granada* distinguishes Almanzor from champions "of the Salvage kind," and his horsemanship at the contest identifies him as one to the manner born, lacking only the pretentious gallantry of the other courtiers. His uniquely irrepressible freedom of spirit is the only condition of his primitive origin which has essentially affected him: "I alone am King of me," he tells Boabdelin, the King of Granada;

> I am as free as Nature first made man,
> 'Ere the base Laws of Servitude began,
> When wild in woods the noble Savage ran. (Pt. 1, I, 34)

Human freedom, as realized in the character of Almanzor, is in fact the subject on which the actions of all the major characters of the play provide a commentary. The Christian conquest of Granada itself is conceived of by the Spanish as a restoration "to freedom and true faith" (Pt. 2, I, 94), the rights of Moorish occupation having in an earlier war been forfeited by Boabdelin in exchange for his personal freedom from the Christians; and although his illegal continuance as the king is technically described as a "freedom" (Pt. 1, I, 37), his unsuitability as ruler has placed both himself and his subjects in the hands of rebellious factions within the city. A "weathercock of State," turned in the first act by the conflicting demands of each faction, Boabdelin is constrained in the exercise of his power, afraid to administer justice or to command. By the end of the first part of the play, his authority has been limited to the walls of the Alhambra.

In Part II, the balance of power has shifted to his subjects, who still further jeopardize his precarious hold upon the throne; and "while People tugg for Freedom, Kings for pow'r,/Both sink beneath some foreign Conquerour" (I, 98). Possessing, but unable to spend, Boabdelin is however no more unhappy as wearer of the crown than as husband of its "fairest Jewel," the virtuous Almahide. Almanzor describes him as a "Miser doom'd to all this store . . . who has all, and yet believes he's poor" (III, 117). Forced by his subjects to recall the hero from exile, he begs Almahide against her better judgment to summon Almanzor's aid, and then he interprets her consent as evidence of her complicity in a "Love-plot." "You should have lov'd me more then to obey," he tells her, and illogically he inveighs against marriage for failing to be the "cure, which Husband's boast,/That, in possession, their desire is lost" (I, 102, 100).

Boabdelin's enslavement is repeated, with variations, in his brother Abdalla; in Abdelmelech, the chief of the Abencerrages; and in Abenamar, the father of Almahide and Ozmyn. Abdalla, who refuses to be the slave of fortune, rebels against Boabdelin, only to become the "sceptered slave" of Lyndaraxa, whose beauties also ensnare and emasculate Abdelmelech. In Abdalla, and in Zulema—whose attempted rape of Almahide is first of all an act of ingratitude—the impulse for honorable action is thwarted by passion: reason, says Abdalla, "like a Captive King, 'tis borne away,/And forc'd to count'nance its own Rebels sway (Pt. 1, III, 47). In Abenamar, on the other hand, not passion but the strict laws of honor inhibit the free expression of natural gratitude and paternal love. Knowing only that he owes the life of his son Ozmyn to the "noble Pity" of a girl he would first raise altars to the virtue of this "visible Divinity" (Pt. 1, IV, 70). But, on learning that she is Benzayda, the daughter of one of the Zegris and his greatest enemy, he calls her birth "a crime past pardon or defense" (Pt. 1, V, 76). Ozmyn has become a "prodigal" son, incurring debts upon the family's honor; and "by meanly taking of the life they gave," he has given Benzayda's family an "advantage," a wrong which can be righted only by Benzayda's death or by Ozmyn's renunciation of her. Later, such honor is recognized as the suppression of the noblest instincts of human nature: as the "errour; that great spirits find,/Which keeps down vertue strugling in the mind" (Pt. 2, IV, 132). Then Abenamar's natural affections are freely released:

> 'Twas long before my stubborn Mind was won;
> But, melting once, I on the suddain run.
> Nor can I hold my headlong kindness more
> Than I could curb my cruel Rage before. (Pt. 2, IV, 132)

Just as the Abdalla-Zulema complication distinguishes the dramatic concept of freedom from license, the Abenamar-Ozmyn complication identifies it with *liberality,* the basic conflict of the play consisting in the opposition not of love and honor or of passion and reason, but of acts of getting and giving: the grasping ambition of Lyndaraxa rides roughshod over the services of her slaves, the jealous possessiveness of Boabdelin abuses Almahide's self-sacrifices, while on the other hand Selin, Ozmyn, and Benzayda vie to outdo each other in generosity in order to satisfy the demands of Abernamar's honor. The most repeated motif of the play is the performance of service and the payment of rewards, and metaphors suggesting the handling and transference of wealth constitute its dominant imagery: Ferdinand is early in the play compared to a "usurer" who "sold" Abenamar's "kindness at a boundless rate,/And then orepaid the debt from his Estate" (Pt. I, 37); Boabdelin speaks as a "Beggar" to his subjects (Pt. 1, I, 36), and enjoys his wealth as does a "Miser" (Pt. 2, III, 117); both Almanzor (Pt. 1, IV, 71) and Benzayda (Pt. 2, IV, 130) are compared to pirates; Ozmyn is censured as a "Prodigal" (Pt. 2, IV, 130); and Almahide, who is a debtor to Almanzor, has yet such a wealth of love for him that, like "frank gamesters," she "must forswear the play" (Pt. 2, V, 155). Image, action, and character thus express the idea that liberality—which by the end of the play appears as a kingly virtue—is the proper action of only a free man.

Almanzor is, of course, the outstanding illustration of human freedom in the play. Like man in the state of nature "Ere the base Laws of Servitude began," he recognizes no ties of allegiance to nation or to ruler, no laws but those made "only for my sake" (I, 34). "When for my self I fight, I weigh the cause," he says in answer to Abdalla's specious claim to the crown (III, 46); thus in the opening argument between the Abencerrages and Zegrys, Almanzor "saw th' opprest, and thought it did belong/To a King's office to redress the wrong" (I, 34). His actions, then, are determined by no rule outside his own sense of justice and are performed without regard for reward. Friendship, however, even exceeds self-assertiveness as a determinant of Almanzor's actions:

> . . . Friendship will admit of no such Laws;
> That weighs by th' lump, and, when the cause is light,
> Puts kindness in to set the Ballance right.
> True, I would wish my friend the juster side:
> But, in th' unjust my kindness more is try'd. (Pt. 1, IV, 46)

Almanzor's greatest "grace," Dryden wrote in the "Dedication" of the play, is his "inviolable faith in his affection" (III, 18), for friendship so conceived imposes the greatest challenge upon virtue and taxes most severly the generosity of an individual.

At the same time, however, the freedom which permits such magnanimity also sanctions injustice. If Almanzor's liberality proves his essential nobility, his rashness in exercising this freedom indicates his unsuitability as a leader. Eugene Waith has recently called attention to the conflict in Almanzor and other "Herculean heroes" of "an opposition to a corrupt world" and an "obligation to an ideal society."[27] But it must be emphasized here that Dryden insists upon Almanzor's role in a real world where rashness in a ruler is as unsatisfactory as an "impotent . . . will" (Pt. 1, V, 84). What Almanzor learns is not obedience to external laws, for that would deprive him of the better part of his virtue, but transcendence of self or "self-mastery" which, as Werner Jaeger states, implies that "moral action originates in the soul of the individual."[28] Since the opportunity for the most noble actions is granted only after painful struggle, Almanzor's relations with Almahide do not constitute a limitation of freedom by the laws of honor, or even the refining of physical love; it is instead the realization and attainment of a greater freedom born of newly discovered inner strength which is consistent with moral law.

All of Almanzor's moral victories or triumphs over self are positive acts of this nature. In Part 1, though he is twice required to relinquish his love for Almahide—"free" her, in other words—these actions are conceived of in terms of heroic daring: in giving her liberty, Almanzor will "dare be wretched not to make her so" (III, 57); and his resolution to live in misery without her is "more to *dare*" than to suffer death (V, 85). In Part 2, his victories are even greater because he is rationally justified to refuse Almahide. Injured by Boabdelin, who has now married Almahide, Almanzor nevertheless accedes to her plea to defend Granada:

> I'le do't: and now I no Reward will have.
>
> . . . .
>
> Spight of my self I'le Stay, Fight, Love, Despair;
> And I can do all this, because I dare. (II, 114)

And at the end, with every conceivable sense of duty to the Moors abrogated by Almahide's decision to leave Boabdelin to join a convent, his continuance as the protector of the Moors amounts to an action which is godlike:

> Listen, sweet Heav'n; and all ye blest above
> Take rules of Vertue from a Mortal love!
> You've raised my Soul. (V, 157)

Almanzor's words, though immodest, are nevertheless justified; for, as Werner Jaeger has said of the Greek mythical heroes, in conforming their endeavors to what is within their powers to obtain, they become, like God, "truly self-sufficient."[29]

IV Aureng-Zebe

If in Almanzor, the heroic character of the protagonist is defined in moral terms—his rashness spiritualized, his passion made to serve primarily a social rather than a private cause—in Aureng-Zebe, the protagonist whose name provides the title of Dryden's next heroic tradegy (1675), it is all but overshadowed by a moral ideal which is inimical to the heroic. Like his predecessors, Aureng-Zebe mounts a throne at the end of the play, but he does so not by means of heroic passion or by the heroic strength which comes of self-mastery, but by virtue of his filial piety: "Receive the Crown your Loialty preserv'd," the Emperor, his father, tells him at the end of the play. This uniqueness is clearly set before us in an early passage which distinguishes Aureng-Zebe's virtues from those of his three brothers. The eldest of these, Dorah, is described as a "bounteous Master, but a deadly Foe," one who "too openly does Love and hatred show"; Sujah, the second son of the Emperor, is a man from whose "valour" one 'should much expect"; and Morat, the youngest, is "too insolent, too much a Brave,/His Courage to his Envy is a Slave" (I, 91)

What is significant here is the fact that those qualities which marked Dryden's earlier heroes as great men—impatience, self-confidence, arrogance, even liberality—are precisely those which make Dorah and Morat (Sujah is disqualified by being "a *Bigot* of the *Persian* Sect") unsatisfactory as successors to the throne. It is upon the virtues of Aureng-Zebe, instead, that the Indian lords place their hopes:

> By no strong passion sway'd,
> Except his Love, more temp'rate is, and weigh'd:
> This *Atlas* must our sinking State uphold;
> In Council cool, but in Performance bold:
> He sums their [his brothers'] Virtues in himself alone,
> And adds the greatest, of a Loyal Son. (I, 91)

Aspiring to both "a Son's and Lover's praise" (I, 100), Aureng-Zebe's conflict is entirely internal. With the patience of a Cordelia, he suffers a father who considers his children "doubly born" slaves (both "Subject and Son"); who unjustly transfers his favor from Aureng-Zebe to his younger half-brother, Morat; and who attempts to rob him of his love, Indamora. And Aureng-Zebe also withstands the temptress Nourmahal's encouragements to rebel against his father's injustice. Jealousy appears to be his only fault, and even this he finally manages to master.

In the Dedication of *The Conquest of Granada*, Dryden expressed his disapproval of a "tame Heroe who never transgresses the bounds of moral vertue," and his preference of a "more exact Image of humane life," a character of "an eccentrique vertue" (IV, 17). Although Aureng-Zebe's jealousy may be the "irregularity" which is meant to humanize him, it is Morat's faults which we recognize as those which are "incident only to great spirits" (IV, 17) and which relate him to Dryden's earlier heroic protagonists: "Yours is a Soul irregularly great,/

Which wanting temper," he is told by Indamora, "yet abounds with heat,"

> So strong, yet so unequal pulses beat.
> As Sun which does through Vapours, dimnly shine:
> What pity 'tis you are not all Divine! (V, 146)

Although, in Almanzor such "amiable imperfections" were, according to Dryden, to be passed over as so many "moles and dimples" on an otherwise beautiful face and although self-assertiveness is the mark of Dryden's earlier heroic protagonists, in Morat, as in Maximin of *The Indian Emperor*, these flaws are identified with personal viciousness. The primitive origins of both Almanzor and Montezuma bred in them a nobility which could not be corrupted by civilization; Morat, however, is described as Hobbes' natural man—as a savage who, since his presence is disruptive in civilization, can exist only in the natural state of perpetual war:

> When thou wert form'd, Heav'n did a Man begin;
> But the brute Soul, by chance, was shuffl'd in.
> In Woods and Wilds thy Monarchy maintain,
> Where valiant Beasts, by force and rapine, reign.
> In Life's next Scene, if Transmigration be,
> Some Bear, or Lion, is reserv'd for thee. (III, 122)

Similarly, as the natural nobility of Almanzor is exemplified in liberality and generous behavior, the natural viciousness of Morat is exemplified in "a mercenary mind" and in actions motivated by self-interest. Impelled by a desire which is commensurate with an "uncontrolled" will, Morat uses his father's unfaithfulness to his mother as the means of securing the throne himself (III, 125); a slave to his emotions, he first spurns the "dull devotion" of filial duty for the pleasures of Melisinda's love (III, 122), only to reject her as "course fare" when his sensual "appetite" discovers the charms of Indamora (IV, 135). Free to do what he wills, though not free to will, Morat rationalizes that "'tis necessary to be great" by any means, that whatever is is right: "Right comes of course, what e'r he was before; Murder and Usurpation are no more" (V, 145). It may be possible to argue, with Eugene Waith, that Dryden, in his treatment of Morat, "maintains an exceedingly delicate balance between the value of heroic energy and the value of control,"[30] that the ideal of heroic virtue in this play is no different from that exemplified in *The Conquest of Granada,* but that it is more sharply defined in its emphasis upon the faults of heroic energy. But Morat appears in the last act to go beyond merely *controlling* his energy. Indamora converts him to a moral conception of greatness: "All Greatness is in Virtue understood," she tells him; " 'Tis onely necessary to be good"; and Morat, in accepting her view, repudiates the code by which he has lived:

> Renown, and Fame, in vain, I courted long;
> And still pursu'd 'em, though directed wrong.
> In hazard, and in toils, I heard they lay;
> . . . .
> Now you have given me Virtue for my guide. (V, 146)

Morat's development appears, therefore, to undermine the "heroic ethos" of Dryden's earlier plays.[31]

Dryden's conception of Aureng-Zebe as the true hero of the play further supports this view. Consistent with the play's emphasis upon Aureng-Zebe's internal struggles, with its interest in the domestic relations of parents and children, and its interpretation of the villain's heroic energy as a form of naturalistic self-interest, the opposing ideal of heroism in the play is conceived of in terms of sensibility—the capacity for feeling the tender emotions of love and for sharing the misfortunes of others. Morat's conversion by Indamora is in fact the awakening, through his love, of sympathy for her suffering (V, 147); and Aureng-Zebe's most difficult victory is his struggle to countenance Indamora's tears and tenderness for Morat. Throughout the play he exhibits what, by the standard of the earlier plays, is a most unheroic sensibility: he weeps before his father (I, 96) and his mistress (IV, 141); forgives his rivals and his enemies (IV, 130); and he justifies Morat's comtemptuous likening of his soul to that of a "Lamb" in contrast to his own "Lion"-like nature (III, 122).

Perhaps, as Arthur Kirsch has argued, this sentimentalizing of the older heroic ideal is also responsible for the tendency toward enjambment in the verse of *Aureng-Zebe,* a tendency which Dryden brought to fulfillment in the blank verse of his next heroic play, *All for Love,* but which is already anticipated in the prologue to the present play. In the prologue, he confesses that he has grown "weary of his long-lov'd Mistris, Rhyme":

"Passion's too fierce to be in Fetters bound,/And, Nature flies him like Enchanted Ground" (IV, 87). If, as Dryden argued in *The Essay of Dramatic Poesy*,[32] rhyme is the most appropriate verse in which to portray the exalted subjects of tragedy, his impatience with it now suggests that his conception of the nature of tragedy has changed.

V All for Love

There are, as many critics of *All for Love* have recognized, more than metrical differences between this play (1677) and Dryden's earlier tragedies. And if, as Kirsch argues, *Aureng-Zebe* is an "important anticipation of the sentimental drama," Antony's apparent surrender of honor "all for love" appears an even stronger indication of the bankruptcy of the older heroic ideal.[33] Of the six principal characters in the play, only Alexas—Cleopatra's cowardly eunuch, and one of Dryden's three additions to Shakespeare's work (the others are Octavia and Ventidius)—is not marked as a figure of tender sensibility. Though colder than Morat's Melisinda, Antony's dutiful wife Octavia arouses such compassion for herself and her children that Dryden, in the preface to the play, feared that it destroyed the sympathy which was reserved for the protagonists (IV, 181). Dolabella is "fit" to speak Antony's farewell to Cleopatra because of his softheartedness: even "to hear a story," he says, "feign'd for pleasure/Of some sad Lover's death, moistens my eyes/And robs me of my Manhood" (IV, 230); and Ventidius, the pattern "of an old true-stampt Roman," confesses that "there's contagion in the tears of Friends" (I, 198). Antony, though "rough in Battel," yet "bears a tender heart" (II, 204), "more pitiful," after victory, "than . . . Praying Virgins left at home" (I, 196). And Cleopatra, whom Shakespeare identified with "the teeming womb of Egypt,"[34] emblematizes herself with the "bleeding hearts" which adorn the ruby bracelet she sends to Antony (II, 209).

This sentimentalizing of character is consistent with Dryden's interest in current critical discussion concerning the nature of tragic pleasure—in particular, whether the pity which tragedy moves in an audience is the pleasurable *vehicle* of the play's instruction, or whether pity is in itself instructive, insensibly moving us "to be helpful to, and tender over, the distressed, which is the noblest and most god-like of moral virtues."[35] Both the former, "fabulist" view, which stressed the total order of the plot as the basis of the moral of the play, and the latter, "affective" view, which maintained that emotions themselves are agents of moral force, were familiar to Dryden. As Eric Rothstein has shown, they might easily have been held by him at the same time.[36]

Such a dual conception of tragedy seems almost necessary in order to understand Dryden's prefatory statement of the "motive" of *All for Love*: "I mean the excellency of the Moral: for the chief persons represented, were famous patterns of unlawful love; and their end accordingly was unfortunate" (IV, 180). Considered as a succession of emotionally painful experiences, each of which conveys to the audience an awareness of the protagonists' error, *All for Love* conforms to Rapin's "affective" hypothesis of tragedy.[37] It is, however, important to recognize that Antony and Cleopatra are heroic as well as tragic lovers, and to this extent our pity is modified by our admiration of them. The world, according to the play's second title, was "*well* lost"; "no Lovers liv'd so great, or dy'd so well," Serapion eulogizes at the end of the play. Clearly distinguished from the debilitating "heroical" humor of Abdalla and the base appetite of Nourmahal, the love of Antony and Cleopatra is best defined, as Eugene Waith notes,[38] by the words of Queen Isabella in *The Conquest of Granada*:

> Love's a Heroique Passion which can find
> No room in any base degenerate mind:
> It kindles all the Soul with Honours Fire,
> To make the Lover worthy his desire. (Pt. 2, I, 96)

In the context of *All for Love*, such a love is opposed to both the coldly rational law and honor of Rome—represented by Antony's one fate, Ventidius—and to the soft luxury and "inglorious ease" of Egypt, represented by his "other fate" (I, 196), Alexas.

The spiritual flame of honorable love is extinguished when we first see Antony in the play. Although we discover in the second act that the cause of this condition is Antony's belief that Cleopatra no longer loves him, to the soldier Ventidius, Antony's "desperate sloth" is the result of his shame at having "disgrac'd the name of Soldier" in his earlier Egyptian revels

with Cleopatra. He is in any case, at this point, neither lover
nor fighter, but merely "a Commoner of Nature" (I, 197).
Ventidius, however, "fires" Antony with the old Roman honor,
not, it should be noted, by convincing him of the dishonor
of his love but by playing upon his knowledge of Antony's just
nature— by tempting his anger in order to receive his pardon, and
at last his concession: "Pr'ythee do not curse her,/And I will
leave her" (I, 203). But Roman honor is not the heroic ideal
of the play, and, in the next act, the hollow sound of Antony's
soldier-bragging betrays his own sense of its inadequacy: "Lead,
my Deliverer," he commands Ventidius; "I long to leave this
Prison of a Town,/To joyn thy Legions; and, in open Field,/Once
more to show my face" (II, 208). Compare with these "brave"
words his words at the end of the act, when, learning that
Cleopatra is "not only Innocent, but Loves" him, he feels that
he has "more than conquer'd Ceasar now":

> Unbar the Gate that looks to *Caesar's* Camp;
> I would revenge the Treachery he meant me:
> And long security makes Conquest easie.
> I'm eager to return before I go;
> For, all the pleasures I have known, beat thick
> On my remembrance: how I long for night. (II, 215-16)

Antony's reconciliation with Cleopatra in this act is not, as
Ventidius believes, a defeat of Roman honor by Egyptian sen-
suality; rather, it is Antony's discovery of a value greater than
either love or honor by his identification of the two. Cleopatra
has not seduced him; she has appealed—as Ventidius had in
Act I—to Antony's sense of justice. To her, his love is reparation
for basely believing she had been a disloyal mistress and a
treacherous ally; to him, it is an act which comprehends "all
that's excellent" in man—"Faith, Honor, Virtue" (II, 216).

Antony's meeting with Cleopatra in the third act, following
his victory over Caesar's forces, describes this ideal of love
as a joining of the divine powers of Venus and Mars:

> Suppose me come from *Phlegraean* Plains,
> Where gasping Gyants lay, cleft by my Sword;
> And Mountain-tops par'd off each other blow,
> To bury those I slew: receive me, goddess:
> Let *Caesar* spread his subtile Nets, like Vulcan;
> In thy embraces I would be beheld
> By Heav'n and Earth at once;

And make their envy what they meant their sport. (III, 217)
Described here in heroic terms, the conduct of Antony and
Cleopatra is an "awful State," the prerogative of only "superior"
gods. As love it is distinguished from the material lust of the
sons of earth, from Egyptian luxury, as honor from the cold
morality of the lesser gods, or from Roman law. As in Dryden's
earlier heroic plays, Antony is a demigod whose potential for
good, until it is brought under control, is inconsistent with the
social order: "Virtue's his path," says Ventidius of him; "but
sometimes 'tis too narrow/For his vast Soul; and then he starts
out wide,/And bounds into a Vice" (I, 194).

But the catastrophe of *All for Love* is precipitated not by
the undisciplined energies of the hero but by the attempts
of Alexas and Ventidius to make Antony conform to conventional
or mutually exclusive limits of love and honor. In Act III,
Ventidius prompts Antony to accept "honourable Terms" for
"an easier peace" with Caesar by honoring his marital obligations
to Octavia. In the next act, Alexas, the custodian of human
passions, directs Cleopatra to feign love for Dolabella in order
"to fire the heart of jealous *Antony*" (IV, 232), a plot which
Ventidius seizes upon to widen the breach between Antony
and Cleopatra. Though tragically involved in the private rivalry
of the soldier and the eunuch, the heroic love of the protagonists
remains impervious to the tug of war waged about it. Cleopatra
confesses her "one minutes feigning" to Dolabella: "Oh, rather
let me lose,/Than so ignobly trifle with his heart" (IV, 235);
and Antony, instead of jealously pursuing Cleopatra, laments
the perfidy of his friend and mistress. But we learn that he
loves her in spite of this when his plan for a final battle—a
desperate attempt with Ventidius to "leave our wond'ring destinies behind"—is cut short by the false report of Cleopatra's
death:

> What should I fight for now? My queen is dead.
> I was but great for her; my Pow'r, my Empire,
> Were but my Merchandise to buy her love. (V, 254)

Antony does indeed escape his human destinies of love and
honor, and paradoxically he is assisted by Alexas' final plot—a
desperate scheme for his own preservation, "no matter what
becomes of *Cleopatra*" (V, 251). Nevertheless Antony's death,
in true heroic fashion, challenges and masters his fate: "Only

thou/Cou'dst triumph o'er thy self," says Cleopatra on finding his body (V, 259); and, in following him she too makes her heroic status secure. In death, they appear to Serapion as two gods seated "in State together . . . giving Laws to half Mankind." We pity Antony and Cleopatra, then, not, as we did Morat, because their heroic power was ultimately destructive, but because human existence imposes tragic limitations upon the aspirations of their heroic power.[39]

CHAPTER 5

Literary and Political Satire

A great poem, the Neoclassicists believed, dealt with a great subject in a good manner; and Dryden, who had served his poetic apprenticeship with the panegyrics to the newly restored king, and then gone on to experiment with the heroic mode in the theater, might next be expected to have produced his epic. Indeed, he wrote of this intention on several occasions, once, in such obscure terms that, as Dr. Johnson noted, "he seems afraid lest his plan [an heroic poem on either King Arthur or Edward the Black Prince] should be purloined."[1] Then, in 1677, Dryden's friend and collaborator Nathaniel Lee suggested that he write an epic on "the troubles of Majestic *CHARLES*," which he significantly likened to the troubles of David:

> Praise Him, as *Cowly* did that *Hebrew* King,
> Thy Theam's as great, do thou as greatly sing.
> Then thou may'st boldly to his favor rise,
> Look down and the base serpent's hiss despise,
> From thund'ring envy safe in Lawrel sit,
> While clam'rous Critiques their vile heads submit
> Condemn'd for Treason at the bar of Wit.[2]

Lee's lines are from his commendatory poem on *The State of Innocence*, Dryden's quasioperatic version of *Paradise Lost*, an interesting example of the heroic impulse of which we are speaking. Indeed, *King Arthur*, when it finally appeared in 1691, and the dramatic celebration of the House of Stuart called *Albion and Albanius*, produced in 1685, were also cast in operatic form, a fact which may indicate the remoteness of Dryden and his age from anything like the true heroic spirit. The spectacle and music of opera appeal to the eye and ear rather than to the mind, and although Dryden made no apology for thus "modernizing" a Classical mode, his defense of "poetical fictions" and heroic rhyme in the "Apology for Heroic Poetry and Poetic License" prefixed to *The State of Innocence* makes explicit the difficulty of honoring the Neoclassical ideals of the heroic and the sublime in an age of rationalism.

One consequence of this Classical-rational dilemma was, as we have seen, the peculiarly sceptical nature of Dryden's criticism, a precarious balance of Neoplatonic critical concepts and of Cartesian criteria of truth. Another, with which we shall be concerned in this chapter, was the characteristic use of satire, burlesque, and verse epistle which has come to be recognized as Augustan. Believing, on the one hand, that epic and tragedy comprised the great literary genres, yet recognizing, on the other, that they could not write them, that what they could write comprised, by Neoclassical standards, a "lower" and less dignified genre, the greatest poets of the period chose, at least on occasion, to do what they could do well and, if necessary, to excuse it with the understanding that they were not aiming at really "great" poetry. Thus, in the preface to *Religio Laici*, Dryden admonishes his critics not to expect "Florid, Elevated and Figurative" language in a poem "design'd purely for Instruction."[3] At the end of the poem he remarks: "Thus have I made my own Opinions clear:/Yet neither Praise expect, nor Censure fear" (11. 451-52).

Satire and the verse epistle had, of course, their own rules; but they were less restrictive than those governing the heroic genres, and permitted the poet "to shift, honorably, from the Beautiful to the Characteristic."[4] For Dryden, moreover, satire did not in theory try to avoid "the Beautiful." Of the two kinds of satire written by the Romans—Horace's urbane laughter at folly in language which is "low" or familiar, and Juvenal's indignant attack upon vice in language suitable to "sublime and lofty thoughts"—Dryden believed the former the better, essaying it, for example, in the character of Zimri (Buckingham) in *Absalom and Achitophel*, a portrait which he later judged to be "worth the whole poem": "If I had railed, I might have suffered for it justly; but I managed my own work more happily, perhaps more dextrously. I avoided the mention of great crimes, and applied myself to the representing of blindsides, and little extravagancies; to which, the wittier a man is, he is generally the more obnoxious."[5] Yet, he confessed, Juvenal is the more personally satisfying and nobler poet, and one ought not discriminate against him for his "pains of numbers" and "loftiness of figures."[6]

In turning to satire, then, Dryden did not repudiate the heroic and the sublime, a view which is further substantiated by his long digression on the epic in "A Discourse concerning . . . Satire." His combination of a "fine raillery" with what Mark Van Doren calls his "huge thoroughness"[7] suggests his honoring of both the *sermo pedestris* of Horace and the noble expression of Juvenal. Even the mock genres are not mockeries of the heroic manner, but rather "elegantly affectionate homage, offered by a writer who finds it irrelevant to his age."[8] *Mac Flecknoe, Absalom and Achitophel,* and *The Medall,* then, constitute what W. K. Wimsatt has happily called a "vacation" from the ideal, "the serious fun which an expressionist theory would call being true to themselves."[9]

It is probably impossible to state with assurance that Dryden the man (who, according to his own and his contemporaries' testimonies, was naturally retiring) was a satirist by temperament; his dispassionate professionalism remains as an everpresent check upon the tendency to generalize from the work to the man himself—even though such generalization is often necessary. Dryden's statement, in his elegy to the satirist John Oldham—"For sure our Souls were near ally'd; and thine/Cast in the same Poetick mould with mine" (I,389)—for all its ring of simple truth, may be nothing more than sincere homage to the dead. It may be sufficient, however, to recognize that in the fiercely competitive world of the Restoration theater, the ability to make one's way before tasteless audiences and jealous detractors was no doubt instinctive, particularly when one's supposed natural diffidence and professional competence may be assumed to have provoked personal attack. Dryden's dramatic prologues and epilogues, written for his own and others' plays, provide ample evidence of the fact that the satirical voice was part of the required stock in trade of the professional man of letters at this time.

As Mark Van Doren says, dramatic prologues and epilogues had become "social events" in the Restoration.[10] Dryden employed these theatrical occasions to initiate commonsense thinking in a world subjected to false wit, spectacle, and farce both in and out of the theater. We, the actors, may cease, and you will "Act your selves the Farce of your own Age" (I, 206), he informs the audience in the prologue to Tate's *The Loyal General* (1679). And in the prologue to Lee's *Caesar Borgia* (1680), he complains that the dramatist is condemned to starve in a world in which the court ("the great *Exchange* of News 'tis hight") usurps the theater: "Would you return to us we dare engage/To show you better Rogues upon the Stage" (I, 204). From the point of view of the still commonplace analogy of the macrocosm world and the microcosm theater, Dryden's references to the public's demand for witless drama become metaphors of the demands of a rebellious populace; thus he tells the scholars at an Oxford "Act" in 1673 that Jonson "owns no Crown" from London audiences ("those Praetorian bands"), "but knows *that* Right is in this Senates hands" (I, 370). The infection of public taste by French "wit" he describes as the symptom of a moral disease—as the inability to distinguish between right and wrong, and the true and the false:

> The Plays that take on our Corrupted Stage,
> Methinks resemble the distracted Age;
> Noise, Madness, all unreasonable Things,
> That strike at Sense, as Rebels do at Kings!
> The stile of Forty One [Year of the rebellion against
>   Charles I] our Poets write,
> And you are grown to judge like Forty Eight [Year of
>   the execution of Charles I].[11]

Such a world may be regarded as both comic and dangerous, for its witlessness allows it to honor a Popish plot as readily as a bad dramatic plot, a Shaftesbury as readily as a Shadwell.

I Mac Flecknoe

In *Mac Flecknoe,* the earliest of Dryden's three great satires, the implicit danger of witlessness is subverted by the narrator's ironic vision of a world in which "dullness" is the norm and by the primary intention of the author to vex rather than to reform a specific individual. Composed perhaps as early as 1678 and circulated in manuscript until pirated in 1682, the poem is now understood to be the culmination of a purely literary quarrel, to which the political implication of the subtitle of the first edition ("A satyr upon the *True-Blew-Protestant*

Poet, T. S.") is probably unauthoritative if not irrelevant. To be sure, "T. S.," or Thomas Shadwell (1642-92), was politically opposed to Dryden's Toryism in 1682; in that year Dryden added him, in the portrait of Og, to the gallery of factious Whigs he contributed to the second part of *Absalom and Achitophel,* Nahum Tate's continuation of Dryden's allegorical account of the contemporary political crisis.

But, as early as 1668 and intermittently over the next decade, Shadwell, a writer of humor-comedy and a self-styled "son" of Ben Jonson, quarreled with Dryden in the prefaces of their respective plays. Though actually little more than innuendo on both sides, the altercation nevertheless touched upon a literary issue which sharply divided the two men: the relative importance in comedy of wit (Dryden's position) and of humour (Shadwell's position), an issue which, for Shadwell, apparently ratified his claim of being Jonson's successor in the tradition of English comedy.[12] The final episode in this prelude to *Mac Flecknoe* was possibly Shadwell's compliment to George Villiers, Duke of Buckingham, in the dedication of his *History of Timon of Athens, the Man-Hater* (1677-78).[13] Buckingham had been the chief author of *The Rehearsal* (1671), that witty dramatic satire of Dryden and of the Restoration theater; and Shadwell's reference to it and to the justness of Buckingham's more recent critical approval of Shadwell's works and censure of others' may well have provided Dryden with sufficient cause to retaliate by making capital of Shadwell's aspirations to literary leadership—in *Mac Flecknoe,* a poem which names Shadwell as the rightful successor to Richard Flecknoe (d. 1687), an Irish writer whose name had become synonymous with bad poetry.

As an expression of Dryden's personal feelings of animosity toward Shadwell, *Mac Flecknoe* succeeds admirably: its victim emerges as a stupid fat man, a bad musician, an ineffectual satirist, and a dull and unoriginal dramatist whose labored efforts at comedy are fit for only the least discriminating of audiences. As such a man, Shadwell may actually have appeared to Dryden, and it is satisfying and perhaps instructive to watch the latter vindicate himself. But great satire is more than an expression of personal feeling, more than lampoon, which Dryden, moreover, believed was an "unlawful" weapon since "we have no moral right on the reputation of other men."[14] Great satire, Maynard

Mack has reminded us, is always in some way fictional and, in that sense, impersonal.[15] In *Mac Flecknoe*, then, Shadwell appears not only as small as Dryden believed him to be—trimmed down to proper size—but smaller than that: he is diminished by his contrast with the important matters suggested by the heroic fable and style of the poem.

The basic absurdity of Shadwell's succession to Flecknoe's place in the hierarchy of poets is compounded by the development of the analogy between Flecknoe and Augustus, between Shadwell and Ascanius and Romulus, and between the determination of a literary succession and a royal succession. The heroic background of the poem is further suggested by means of conscious echoes of Cowley (ll. 72-3, 76-7), Waller (ll. 38-49), and Virgil (ll. 108-11, 134-38), and sustained throughout the poem by dignified but at times archaic diction and occasional triplets. The following passage, describing the place of Shadwell's coronation, may serve to illustrate the art of the whole poem:

> Close to the Walls which fair *Augusta* bind,
> (The fair *Augusta* much to fears inclin'd)
> An ancient fabrick, rais'd t'inform the sight,
> There stood of yore, and *Barbican* it hight:
> A watch Tower once; but now, so Fate ordains,
> Of all the Pile an empty name remains.
> From its old Ruins Brothel-houses rise,
> Scenes of lewd loves, and of polluted joys.
> Where their vast Courts the Mother-Strumpets keep,
> And, undisturb'd by Watch, in silence sleep.
> Near these a Nursery erects its head,
> Where Queens are form'd, and future Hero's bred:
> Where unfledg'd Actors learn to laugh and cry,
> Where infant Punks their tender Voices try,
> And little *Maximins* the Gods defy. (ll. 64-78)

Augusta might well be inclined to fears (a topical allusion to London's fear of a Popish plot); Barbican, its ancient fortress is now "an empty name," its armed "Watch" having left it as a retreat in which prostitutes may practice their trade. With Barbican, Dryden associates the king, that other defender of human rights and values. But kingship and heroism are now also empty names, the roles which children "learn" in the "Nursery," a school of dramatics established to prohibit "obscene, scandalous, or offensive" plays,[16] but now ironically a convenience to the "scenes of lewd loves" in which the juvenile actors were begotten. The passage makes us see that Shadwell's posture as poet-king is unreal, theatrical—an absurdity as great as the contradictory "little *Maximins*" of the anticlimactic third line of the triplet.

In *Astraea Redux* and in *Annus Mirabilis*, Dryden's serious attempts at heroic poetry, use was made of Biblical as well as Classical materials to portray the ideal of kingship: Charles was depicted as both just and merciful, as a hero and a savior. A corresponding pattern of Biblical allusion supports the Classical motif in Dryden's mock-heroic poem. Near the beginning of *Mac Flecknoe*, Flecknoe explains to Shadwell that

> *Heywood* and *Shirley* were but Types of thee,
> Thou last great Prophet of Tautology:
> Even I, a dunce of more renown than they,
> Was sent before but to prepare thy way;
> And coursly clad in *Norwich* Drugget came
> To teach the Nations in thy greater name. (ll. 29-34)

If Heywood, Shirley, and later in the poem (l. 87) Dekker (Dryden's list of bad dramatists from the preceding age) represent Old Testament foreshadowings ("Types") of Christ, if Flecknoe, like John the Baptist, came out of the wilderness (Ireland) in his coarse rags (Druggett) to teach in Christ's name and prepare His way, then Shadwell is the Word Incarnate, the "last great Prophet of Tautology." Accordingly, the account of Shadwell's royal procession through the city parodies the triumphant entry of Christ into Jerusalem—"scatter'd Limbs of mangled Poets" and the pages of Heywood, Shirley, and Ogleby replacing the branches of palm and garments of the original:

> Rows'd by report of Fame, the Nations meet,
> From near *Bun-Hill*, and distant *Watling-street*.
> No *Persian* Carpets spread th' Imperial way,
> But scatter'd Limbs of mangled Poets lay:
> From dusty shops neglected Authors come,
> Martyrs of Pies, and Reliques of the Bum. (ll. 96-101)

And at the end of the poem, much the same significance may be attached to the allusion to the ascent into heaven of Elijah (another prophet of the coming of Christ)[17] and to his bestowal upon Elisha of a double portion of his spirit by letting fall his mantle:

> . . . down they sent the yet declaiming Bard.
> Sinking he left his Drugget robe behind,

> Born upwards by a subterranean wind.
> The Mantle fell to the young Prophet's part,
> With double portion of his Father's Art. (11. 213-17)

Here, of course, Flecknoe descends rather than ascends, the Drugget mantle rises from below, and Shadwell-Elisha is blessed with a "double portion" of dullness!

In spite of its origin in personal animus, *Mac Flecknoe* is first of all a brilliantly comic poem, an example of the art or "*Genius*" which Dryden believed "will force its own reception in the World . . . even while it Hurts."[18] It would not have been difficult to render Shadwell as nothing more than a contemptible poetaster, "to call rogue and villain, and that wittily," as Dryden says in the "Discourse concerning . . . Satire"; and in the portrait of Og, Shadwell in fact appears as one in whom "every inch that is not Fool is Rogue."[19] Through its playful use of heroic materials, however, *Mac Flecknoe* replaces the viciousness of lampoon with what Ian Jack calls "ironic sympathy" and a "mischievous joy in contemplation."[20] We pity the comic little man made smaller by thinking he is big, but we are also excited by the thought that really important things might get to be as bad as the poem makes them seem. Our laughter at Shadwell does not let us forget that as king, Mac Flecknoe was "sworn by his *Syre* a mortal Foe to *Rome* . . . Ne'er to have peace with Wit, nor truce with Sense" (11. 113, 117); and that, as the Messiah, he came to *save* the world from the same: to be "a scourge of Wit, and flayle of Sense" (1. 89). The health of a nation's literature, the poem reminds us, is an index of the health of the nation itself, a fact of which we are reminded by the only line of the poem which is extraneous to its fable—the sole parenthetical statement in the poem (1. 65); London is "much to fears inclin'd." In the end, then, our laughter is not destructive, but instructive; and the satirist is "no more an Enemy to the Offendour, than the Physician to the Patient, when he prescribes harsh Remedies to an inveterate Disease."[21]

II Absalom and Achitophel

By November, 1681, when *Absalom and Achitophel* appeared, the vague fear of a Popish plot had reached its flood and receded. For a time it had been replaced by a more definite threat of internal subversion in the person of Charles' brother, the Cath-

olic James, Duke of York. Opinion about his fittingness as successor divided the public into Exclusionist and Successionist,
Whig and Tory. But Charles' thwarting in March the passage of
the Exclusion Bill and the arrest in July of Shaftesbury, the chief
fomentor of the opposition, constituted a reaffirmation of monarchical authority and at least a temporary restoration of its
guarantee of peace and order. As a celebration of the king's victory, *Absalom and Achitophel* is a heroic poem; and its final lines
echo the triumphant mood of *Astraea Redux* and *Annus Mirabilis*:

> Henceforth a Series of new time began,
> The mighty Years in long Procession ran:
> Once more the Godlike *David* was Restor'd,
> And willing Nations knew their Lawfull Lord. (11. 1028-31)

This poem has frequently been likened to a "miniature epic" or,
better—since it is not "complete" in the epic sense—to "an episode
out of a potential epic."[22] But although it does not render a judgment—since Shaftesbury was awaiting trial at the time the poem
was composed—it provides as its subject the materials for judgment: the poetic contrast of the spokesmen of two opposed political theories, depicted so as to arouse, on the one hand, the
reader's admiration and sympathy and, on the other, his contempt, a design which was well suited to one who regarded satire as a "species of heroic poetry."[23]

At the center of *Absalom and Achitophel* is the conception
of order as hierarchy or degree with its concomitant principles
of rational law and balance. Man's enjoyment of the good, it implies, consists in his limiting his powers to the sphere to which
God assigned them, his enjoyment of civil rights in his subordi-
nating the self to kings ("the God-heads Images" [1. 792]) and
the laws of magistrates. Obedience to such law assumes reason
or that balance of physical "humours" which constitutes order in
man; to attempt to change one's place in the social order is to
disrupt the mutual dependence of all things, a self-injury which
amounts to "publick Lunacy" (1. 788)—"For who can be secure
of private Right,/If Sovereign sway may be dissolv'd by might?"
(11. 779-80). Literary tradition afforded two classic types of
rebellion against order: Satan, whose crime was conceived as a
form of madness caused by ambitious pride; and Achitophel,
who, though historically the counselor of the rebellious Absalom

rather than a rebel himself, became in the Civil War years another name for "the crafty politician," and, at the time of the disaffection of Monmouth (a natural Absalom to Charles' David), for Lord Shaftesbury,[24] the instigator of the abortive attempt to shake "a setled Throne" (1. 796). For the fable of the poem that Dryden was writing in the weeks preceding Shaftesbury's trial in 1681, the Biblical narrative of Absalom's rebellion against David (with the role of Achitophel psychologically deepened by association with the arch-rebel Satan) was then an obvious choice.

Not the least advantage of the Biblical fable was its familiarity as a commentary on the contemporary situation, a fact which permitted an economy in the formal development of the plot and a concentration, for both satiric and heroic purposes, upon character portraits and upon the ethical significance they embody. The portraits are again used in the three principal parts of the poem—a prologue (11. 1-227) and two semi dramatic acts (11. 228-722; 811-1031)—as a unifying device. In the prologue, all but one of the principal agents of the poem are introduced: the "Headstrong, Moody" Jewish populace (the English) (11. 45-84); the Jebusites or Catholics (11. 85-149); the innocent and beautiful Absalom (11. 17-44); and the false Achitophel (11. 150-227). The second section offers the portraits of the rebellious faction and their "chiefs" (11. 491-681). Placed between the scene of Absalom's temptation by Achitophel (11. 230-490) and the fallen Absalom's rebellious address to the people (11. 698-722), this gallery of fools is a bitterly satirical commentary not only on the general nature of faction but also on Absalom's innocence: "Surrounded thus with Friends of every sort,/Deluded *Absalom*, forsakes the Court" (11. 682-83). Following a transitional essay against innovation (11. 753-810), the third part offers a contrasting gallery of the friends of the king (11. 811-932), and, finally, David's invocation of the law as the restoration of order.

Unlike the static portraits of the other characters, the image of David, the real hero of *Absalom and Achitophel*, develops dramatically throughout the poem: in the constant allusions to the alliance of kingship and divinity, and in the references to David's indulgence of Absalom and his clemency to his enemies —the latter a kingly quality, though interpreted by Achitophel as fear or the desire to live in irresponsible ease. David's appearance at the end of the poem, flanked by the portraits of loyal subjects and a pious son (Ormond's, the Earl of Ossory—11. 829ff.), has thus the effect both of discrediting his enemies and of justifying his determination to restore order.

Dryden's conservative faith in the king as the proprietor of law and order in the state—his consistent horror of the instability of democracy—was, it is now recognized, the logical position to be taken by one who, in speculative literary criticism, described himself as a philosophical sceptic. If, in questions of literary theory, reason must be content with knowledge of only a probable order—a kind of knowing which is, however, sufficient for the tentative procedures of the critic—how much more dangerous are its attempts at experimentation with the very foundations of social welfare and how much wiser it is to rest upon the only kind of certainty which is available in this area—the knowledge of those social institutions which have worked in the past.

Dryden believed, with Montaigne, "that an honest man ought to be contented with that form of government, and with those fundamental constitutions of it, which he received from his ancestors, and under which himself was born."[25] Change implies the repudiation of values. Is it conceivable, the narrator asks, that people can "give away/Both for themselves and Sons, their Native sway?" (11. 759-60). The law which invests the king with power also insures the liberty of the subject; it is a law which need not be affirmed in each generation; it is a "resuming Cov'nant," binding on all posterity, as Adam's fall has "damned us all" (11. 765-74). The reference to "our Fathers fall" and the allusion to Covenant theology is significant here. It reminds the reader that the Eden of the present would be a natural anarchy —"where all have Right to all" (1. 794)—were it not for an uninterrupted succession of royal sovereignty, a new Covenant of Grace in which the king's sacrifice for his subjects is also the reason for the subject's obedience to his king. Thus to "make Heirs for Monarks" is to decree for God (1.758), an act of blasphemy as well as treason since it disturbs the order of the universe:

All other Errors but disturb a State;
But Innovation is the Blow of Fate.
. . . .

> To change Foundations, cast the Frame anew,
> Is work for Rebels who base Ends pursue:
> At once Divine and Humane Laws controul;
> And mend the Parts by ruine of the Whole. (11. 799-808)

Notwithstanding such compelling reasons for obedience, the Jews "as ever try'd th' extent and stretch of grace" (1. 46). Experimenting with Gods "of every shape and size" (1. 49), these "*Adam*-wits" (1. 51) have broken their Covenant with the true God, and in doing so they fell into the anarchy of "Natures state" (1. 794). The English, then, are temperamentally predisposed to rebellion; and, in associating the current political unrest with the behavior of the preceding generation, Dryden justifies his conservative distrust of human nature. A "Headstrong, Moody, race" (1. 45), the English are by nature melancholic, an unsettled temperament which, through excessive heat and black bile, tends to subordinate reason to an overactive imagination and to the fervor of religious enthusiasm—energies which emphasize the individual rather than the social nature of man:

> These *Adam*-wits, too fortunately free,
> Began to dream they wanted libertie;
> And when no rule, no president was found
> Of men, by Laws less circumscrib'd and bound,
> They led their wild desires to Woods and Caves,
> And thought that all but Savages were Slaves. (11. 51-56)

Although these lines refer to the rebels who exiled Charles I, their sons who "imagine" a healthy state diseased, and who "take pains Contingent mischiefs to foresee" (11. 756-57), are no less deceived by an uncontrolled fancy. Moreover, the atrabilious leaders of the faction, though endowed with too much "common Sense" to swallow "unchew'd" the allegations of a Popish plot, are nevertheless involuntarily *moved* by it. Their minds are excessively stimulated to try, without thought of the consequences, what is unwise or impossible:[26]

> . . . as when raging Fevers boyl the Blood,
> The standing Lake soon floats into a Flood;
> And every hostile Humour, which before
> Slept quiet in its Channels, bubbles o'r:
> So, several Factions from this first Ferment,
> Work up to Foam, and threat the Government. (11. 136-41)

It is clearly such an interpretation of character which Dryden wishes to make of Shaftesbury in the portrait of Achitophel, one whose personality and career provide living proof of the "thin Partitions" dividing wit and madness:

> A fiery Soul, which working out its way,
> Fretted the Pigmy Body to decay:
> And o'r inform'd the Tenement of Clay.
> A daring Pilot in extremity;
> Pleas'd with the Danger, when the Waves went high
> He sought the Storms; but for a Calm unfit,
> Would Steer too nigh the Sands, to boast his Wit. (11. 156-62)

We are made to feel in these lines that, although Achitophel-Shaftesbury would be a valuable aid to the king (and Dryden devotes some ten lines to his ability as a judge [11. 186ff.]), he cannot be trusted with power. Like the populace whose weaknesses he knows so well, Achitophel is also subject to *motion* and is committed to short views which sacrifice the blessings of his present state to the uncertainties of change. Who but a madman, the narrator asks, would so punish himself to gain what will become merely a legacy to "that unfeather'd, two Leg'd thing, a Son" (1. 170)? Quite apart from the constitutional issues involved in Shaftesbury's actions, Dryden's interpretation of his character in the portrait of Achitophel is an effective appeal to the reader to follow David, the voice in the poem of reason and sanity.

Supporting the psychological and political contrast of David and Achitophel is the contrast of David as the annointed of God—the spokesman and representative of divine order in the world—and of Achitophel as the Satanic rebel whose pride and ambition seek to overthrow this order. In Dryden's Biblical source (2 *Samuel*, xiv-xviii), Achitophel plays the subordinate role of advisor to Absalom. In *Absalom and Achitophel*, however, Achitophel is the real instigator of the plot against David; and his relations with Absalom suggest nothing more clearly than diabolic temptation: "Believe me, Royal Youth," he says in words described as *venomous* (1. 229), "thy Fruit must be,/Or gather'd Ripe, or rot upon the Tree" (11. 25-51). Dryden was no doubt happy in finding this means of condemning Charles' enemy and of sidestepping the need to judge his son. And in his prefatory "To the Reader," he thus justifies having drawn the character of Absalom "too favourably": "since the most excellent Natures

are always the most easy; and, as being such, are the soonest
perverted by ill Counsels, especially when baited with Fame
and Glory; 'tis no more a wonder that he withstood not the
temptations of *Achitophel,* than it was for *Adam,* not to have
resisted the two Devils; the Serpent, and the Woman" (I, 216).
Accordingly there are some Adamic touches in the treatment of
the beautiful and innocent Absalom,[27] as, for example, in the
transitional passage preceding his first reply to the seductions of
the temptor:

> Th' Ambitious Youth, too Covetous of Fame,
> Too full of Angells Metal in his Frame;
> Unwarily was led from Vertues ways;
> Made Drunk with Honour, and Debauch'd with Praise.
> Half loath, and half consenting to the Ill,
> (For Loyal Blood within him strugled still). (11. 309-14)

Like Satan, Achitophel is "resolv'd to Ruine or to Rule the State"
(1. 174); and his nomination and his support of Absalom are
merely ways of seizing power himself. Absalom recommends
himself not by virtue of his royal blood or his popularity (the
argument by which he is made to seem a blessing to Israel), but
because "his Title [was] not allow'd" (1. 224). Achitophel wishes to deprive David of power, to draw off "Kingly power . . .
to the dregs of a Democracy," and to do this he must support
one whose claim to kingship is specious and whose right depends
entirely upon the wishes of the people (11. 224-27); Absalom, we
are told, "glides unfelt into their secret hearts" (1. 693).

The line just quoted—an ironic allusion to that faith in Christ
which sustains the hearts of men—views the betrayal of Absalom
as a national rather than as merely a personal tragedy; for the
Jews are about to desert David, Christ's Old Testament prototype, and to follow Absalom, a false Messiah whose has succumb-
ed to Satan's temptations. In *Astraea Redux* and in *Annus Mirabilis,* Dryden had interpreted Charles' restoration as the beginning of an age of peace, justice, and mercy comparable to the
Golden Age mentioned by Virgil and long identified with the
coming of Christ. It is significant that much the same language
used by Dryden to deify Charles in those early poems is here
used by Achitophel in his flattery of Absalom:

> Auspicious Prince! at whose Nativity
> Some Royal Planet rul'd the Southern sky;

Thy longing Countries Darling and Desire;
Their cloudy Pillar, and their guardian Fire:
Their second *Moses*, whose extended Wand
Divides the Seas, and shews the promis'd Land:
Whose dawning Day, in every distant age,
Has exercis'd the Sacred Prophets rage:
The Peoples Prayer, the glad Deviners Theam,
The Young-mens Vision, and the Old mens Dream!
Thee, *Saviour*, Thee, the Nations Vows confess
And, never satisfi'd with seeing, bless. (11. 230-41)

Here again is the star announcing the long prophesied arrival of a savior who will show the New Testament Canaan to the Jews; and with it, in the cloud and fire, "the visible signs of the protecting presence of God the Son."[28] Absalom's acceptance from Achitophel of the role of savior, his denial of the sovereignty of David, is an ironic parody of Satan's temptation of Christ in the wilderness—one which Dryden, in the temptation scene which follows it, underscores by echoing Milton's version of the event in *Paradise Regained*. Rebellion against the king is thus the perversion of a divine plan for salvation in the world of fallen man. Just as Adam's sin would have forfeited salvation for all men had God not offered his Covenant of Grace, so, by Absalom's breaking of that "resuming Cov'nant" of successive kingship, men would have given away "both for themselves and Sons, their Native sway" and left themselves "Defensless, to the Sword/Of each unbounded Arbitrary Lord" (11. 759-74). David's long delayed determination to deal with his enemies completely justifies Dryden's reference at the end of the poem to Virgil's announcement of a new Golden Age, a return of a savior who will redeem men from anarchy.

III The Medall

The form and tone of *Absalom and Achitophel* testify to Dryden's confidence in the continuance of Tory fortunes after Charles' dissolution of the Oxford exclusionist parliament and the imprisonment of Shaftesbury: Israel had been saved from an evil time by a king who, after all, merely resumed the authority which, in parental indulgence, he had temporarily suspended. And David's presence in the poem as the conventional symbol of heroic powers is evidence of the currency and validity of a "conservative myth," a public faith, as Bernard Schilling defines it, in "an authority beyond any appeal, whose right to speak is divine and clearly known to be final."[29] The acquittal of Shaftesbury by a London jury in November, 1681, was then both disillusioning and frightening to the Tories. It meant the loss of traditional values, and the apparent triumph of government by majority rule over the established order of the king and the law, of interest and might over right. For Dryden, the Whigs' victory--and their commemoration of it with a medal bearing Shaftesbury's portrait—was a failure of reason among the populace, the coming true of his earlier grotesque vision of a land in which folly (now as an evil potential, however) was the norm. His response was not another *Mac Flecknoe*, but *The Medall* (1682), "A Satyre Against Sedition," addressed, along with a prefatory "Epistle to the Whigs," to those businessmen of London who had participated in the celebration of Shaftesbury's release and who, in so doing, had contributed to their own ruin by debasing the spiritual coin of the realm.

As a statement of conservative thought and as a satirical portrait of Shaftesbury and the Whigs, *The Medall* has suffered by comparison with *Absalom and Achitophel*; but insofar as the latter was specifically described by Dryden as a "poem" (a verse narrative which "imitates something beyond what simply is," and to that extent "becomes free to make a general criticism of life"[30]), it is actually not comparable to *The Medall*, which he describes as a "satyre." At the beginning of 1682, Dryden and his Tory friends could no longer merely acquiesce in a myth of conservatism. London's celebration of Shaftesbury's acquittal was itself a blow against monarchy; and, from beginning to end, *The Medall* expresses a sense of critical urgency:

> That Kings can doe no wrong we must believe:
> None can they doe, and must they all receive?
> Help Heaven! or sadly we shall see an hour,
> When neither wrong nor right are in their pow'r. (11. 135-38)

"To hear an open Slander is a Curse;/But not to find an Answer, is a worse": so Dryden translated the lines (11. 1064-65) from Ovid with which *The Medall* ends. In his "answer" to the Whigs, Dryden invoked the lampooner's privilege of exacting revenge from the seditious; and, in doing so, he more narrowly limited himself to the contemporary circumstances which called it forth than he had in the two preceding poems. But *The Medall* is not merely an "excuse" for revenge; satire justifies itself, Dryden believed, by making examples of vicious men. Satire is a virtuous "duty" which requires objectivity and art, for "there can be no pleasantry where there is no wit" and "no impression can be made where there is no truth for the foundation."[31]

The textural richness of *The Medall*, though seldom recognized as much more than contemporary allusion, is comparable to that of the two poems just discussed, as well as to that of Dryden's early heroic poems written at the Restoration. The Shaftesbury medal, for example, functions not only literally but also metaphorically and symbolically to establish the folly of London. It is, first of all, evidence of the city's admiration of Shaftesbury, "a Monster" who is nevertheless "The Favourite of the Town," rivaling the affection of "*English* Ideots" for fairs and the theater (11. 1-5). Throughout the satire, as in *Astraea Redux*, the love of the people for a hero is a general image of the *mutual* interest which unites a nation and its rulers. The reference to Shaftesbury's pretensions to the Polish throne (1. 11) and to his "regal Place" (the tower depicted on the medal) indicates, then, that London's enthusiasm for Shaftesbury is tantamount to an acceptance of him as king. Metaphorically, the medal represents a religious "Idol" (1. 7), an image of a false God ("golden to the sight," but "base within" [11. 8-9]) in whom the people "*rejoyce*" on their "new Canting Holiday" (11. 14-17). Finally, the medal is a symbol of "conterfeit" coinage (1. 9); for to join the Duke's party is to assume the prerogatives of the king, to "clip his regal Rights" (1. 229), the real source of national prosperity. Ironically paralleling the city's reaction to the medal of Shaftesbury is the objective portrait of the man, given next in terms of his "ever-changing Will" (1. 24). The city's darling appears now as a gross lecher whose "open lewdness he cou'd ne'er disguise" to the Puritans (1. 37), even though he had managed to conceal the "Fiend" within the "Saint-like mould" he cast for himself (1. 33). Here, too, the city's regard for Shaftesbury as its source of wealth and power is seen to rest upon his appeal to the citizens' own interests, a false power that "leapst o'r all eternal truths" (1. 94) and that dictates action which appears true only for as "long we please it shall continue so" (11. 107-8).

Twice illustrated as a blindness to the gross discrepancies between appearance and reality, the sedition of London is next conceived of as a venereal infection contracted from Shaftesbury, the lover of the people. His "blandishments" have "whor'd" a loyal land, "broke the Bonds she plighted to her Lord" (11. 256-59). Moreover, as the disorder caused by the breaking of the covenant of successive monarchy is a curse to all succeeding generations, so, as a result of the present infection, "all must curse the Woes that must descend on all" (1. 262). Religion, the cure of spiritual malaise in the nation (and hence a form of *"Mercury"* which was used to combat venereal disease), is itself tainted by interest (11. 263-64): the Whigs "rack ev'n Scripture to confess their Cause" and "make it speak whatever Sense they please" (11. 156, 163). At last the brain is infected (1. 266), and the nation succumbs to the madness of anarchy in the state, in the church, and in the marketplace. The power which rests on the instability of interest (Dryden never allows us to forget that the Whigs are largely shopkeepers and London the "great *Emporium* of our Isle" [1. 167]) is self-destructive:

> In Gospel phrase their Chapmen they betray:
> Their Shops are Dens, the Buyer is their Prey.
> The Knack of Trades is living on the Spoyl;
> They boast, ev'n when each other they beguile.
> Customes to steal is such a trivial thing,
> That 'tis their Charter, to defraud their King.
> All hands unite of every jarring Sect;
> They cheat the Country first, and then infect. (11. 191-98)

The outcome is inevitable; "inborn Broyles" will engage the factions:

> The swelling Poyson of the sev'ral Sects,
> Which wanting vent, the Nations Health infects
> Shall burst its Bag; and fighting out their way
> The various Venoms on each other prey. (11. 294-97)

England, which will admit arbitrary power in neither one nor the many, will ultimately exhaust itself in "wild Labours" and recline again upon "a rightful Monarch's Breast" (11. 321-22).

CHAPTER 6

Religious Poems

On the basic issue of the role of reason in religion, three positions were taken in Dryden's century. At one extreme stood the Deist, who rejected supernatural revelation with the assurance that the natural light of human reason afforded all that was necessary for salvation. At the other extreme stood the fideist, who as summarily rejected the authority of human reason in his total surrender to faith in revelation. This anti-rationalist view, though never sanctioned by the Roman Church, was customarily identified as the Catholic position; it was also, however, associated with the Puritan sects, who sought religious authority in the irrational communications of a "Private Spirit." Between these two extremes the Anglican traveled a *via media* which recognized no essential incompatability between reason and revelation; the former, or "right reason," as it was called, provided not only such basic religious truths as the Deist recognized but also the motivation for and the means of understanding the supernatural truths of revelation which, since the incarnation of the Word in Christ, were absolutely necessary for salvation. By following the Scriptures, the Anglican believed, each man might find his way to Heaven, for their clarity was sufficient in all but matters of secondary importance. And for the understanding of these, the Anglican could rely on the judgment of those scholars who have spent "their whole time principally in the study of things divine, to the end that in these more doubtful cases their understanding might be a light to direct others."[1]

Where Dryden stood in relation to these positions has been a matter of considerable interest to scholars, since over his lifetime he appears to have run almost the entire gamut of belief, moving from Puritanism to Anglicanism and, in 1685, to Catholicism. Since 1934, when Louis Bredvold's influential study, *The Intellectual Milieu of John Dryden* was published, Dryden's contact with an intellectual tradition of philosophical scepticism has been regarded as an increasingly important influence upon his thought. Evidence of the characteristic humility of this sort of scepticism has already been recognized in the critical objectivity which informs Dryden's disinterested survey of ancient and modern literary opinion in *An Essay of Dramatic Poesy*. From a similiar point of view derives his distrust of the individualistic tendencies of Whiggism and his compensating acquiesence in the system of traditional values embodied in the idea of monarchical government. Realistically aware of the errors to which pride in human reason may lead, and honestly recognizing the inconsistencies in his own rational processes, Dryden seems gradually to have come to value the testimony of working institutions more than his own reason. Clearly, his complete identification of the nation's interests with those of the king indicates the expression of this side of his temperament. It is doubtful that Dryden ever felt closely identified with the Puritan government with which his family had sympathized: but, even if he had, his Toryism and his subsequent conversion to Catholicism may be viewed as evidence less indicative of an unprincipled character than of one which moved consistently toward the conservative position from which the philosophical sceptic normally regards the disturbing changes of his world.

I *Anglican Fideism and* Religio Laici

The roots of seventeenth-century philosophical scepticism are in the *Pyrrhonic Hypotyposes* of Sextus Empiricus, a summary of the thought of Pyrrho of Elis and other ancients on the uncertainty of human knowledge and, consequently, the untenability of ethical dogmatism. Rediscovered in the sixteenth century, this brand of scepticism, or Pyrrhonism as it came to be called, was absorbed by the medieval conception of the fallen nature of man and the Augustinian doctrine of grace, and was thus employed to defend the authority of faith against the encroachments of individual judgment—except in Protestant climates where opposition to Roman Catholic authority was made by an appeal to individual reason.[2] The Anglican Sir Thomas Browne's *Religio Medici* (1643)—one title among many like it which may have suggested Dryden's title of *Religio Laici*—was Pyrrhonistic in its subordination of reason to faith. Though a work of great popularity during the century, it "diverged widely," according to

Professor Bredvold, "from the rationalism which more and more characterized Anglican thought in the century of Chillingworth and Tillotson."[3] In England, then, the fideist, anti-rationalist argument might serve to liberate faith or perhaps to oppose such extremist views as those of the Socinians and the Deists, but in France it was employed as a means of undermining the authority of the Scriptural basis of Protestantism.[4]

A related attack upon Protestantism was the publication in 1678 of Father Simon's *Histoire critique du Vieux Testament*, a work of higher criticism which pointed out the unreliability of the Biblical text, and thereby showed the necessity of an oral tradition of interpretation as the basis of authority in the Church. In its English translation (1682) by Henry Dickinson, the book no doubt alarmed many Anglicans; and it drew forth at least one appeal (by John Evelyn to Dr. Fell, the Bishop of Oxford[5]) for a controverting defense of the principles of Anglicanism. In November, 1682, appeared Dryden's *Religio Laici*, "written for an ingenious young Gentleman my Friend; upon his Translation of *The Critical History of the Old Testament*."[6] Ostensibly written as a "Confession" of his own faith (Anglicanism), the poem is thus also a vindication of the adequacy of Scripture as an authority in religion. According to Bredvold, however, the thought of the poem is essentially fideistic, and its similarity to his later defense of Catholicism in *The Hind and the Panther* (1687) indicates that, probably without realizing it, Dryden "was already in 1682 far along on the road to the Roman communion."[7]

In support of this view, Bredvold points to such evidence as the direct attack upon reason in the poem's opening lines and in its criticism of Deism, as well as to its acquiescence in the plain but necessary truths of Scripture and to the authority of the Church Fathers in its criticism of the Protestant sects. Acceptance of the Fathers and of Scripture, a common Anglican compromise which substituted "a judicious and learned individualism for the extravagant individualism of the Private Spirit," would be relinquished in the later Catholic poem for the stronger authority of an infallible Church; but Bredvold finds that even in *Religio Laici* the idea of such a strong authority—notwithstanding the poet's Anglican argument to the contrary—was appealing: "Such an *Omniscient* Church, we wish indeed," Dryden wrote; "'Twere worth *Both Testaments,* and cast in the *Creed*" (11. 282-83).[8]

As a means of explaining Dryden's subsequent conversion to Catholicism and of bringing into focus the significance of his self-avowed scepticism, the fideistic reading of *Religio Laici* is indeed valuable, a fact attested to by its wide acceptance among Dryden scholars. But its acceptance has not been unanimous. The late Edward Niles Hooker objected to the imputation of a fideistic repudiation of reason to one as "habitually ratiocinative" as Dryden. He argued that the poem was trying to right the balance of "constricting dogma" and "corroding scepticism" by establishing not only the limits but also the "scope" of reason, and that Dryden's own scepticism was, like Plutarch's opposed to both dogmatic system-making and to Pyrrhonic scepticism.[9]

In 1961, the independent studies of Thomas Fujimura and Elias Chiasson arrived at the same doubt of Dryden's alleged fideism and scepticism, and advanced instead readings of *Religio Laici* as an Anglican poem—in the tradition of Christian humanism, according to Chiasson, or colored by Arminianism in Fujimura's view. Both argue that the poem should be read in the context of Anglican attitudes toward the authority of reason and tradition. Reason, says Fujimura, had by Dryden's time, become the instrument not of apprehending (which was now the function delegated to faith) but of weighing and consenting to religious truths; moreover, in combating the private spirit of the Puritans, the Anglican risked pursuing his argument to its logical consequence, rational theology.[10] The opening lines of the poem reveal, then, not Dryden's fideism but the difficulty experienced by all Anglicans in maintaining the concept of *right* reason in an age of Deistic rationalism; they state nothing more than the orthodox Christian belief "that reason without faith cannot come to the fullness of Christian truth."[11] If anything, Fujimura adds, Dryden is more, not less rationalistic than the orthodox Anglican, for he appears to assert "the adequacy of natural reason for salvation" in the case of heathen who do not have the benefit of revelation.[12] Futhermore, Dryden will accept tradition only where it is consistent with the testimony of Scripture; and, as to his hankering after authority, the lines stating that "an *Omniscient* Church . . . were worth *Both Testaments,* and cast in the Creed" (11. 282-83) are ironic; they express "not yearning for but dismissal of the reality behind the principle of Catholic infallibility."[13]

Certainly, these arguments make it no longer possible to exaggerate the rationalism of seventeenth-century Anglicanism, to oversimplify its differences from Catholicism, or to accept unquestionably Professor Bredvold's conclusion that Dryden was already *far* along on the road to Catholicism in 1682. Dryden appears to have been sincerely anxious to make the poem acceptable to Anglican readers; as to its opinions, "whatever they are," he writes in the long preface, "I submit them with all reverence to my Mother Church, accounting them no further mine, than as they are Authoriz'd, or at least, uncondemn'd by her." And, to secure himself on this side, he adds, "I have us'd the necessary Precaution, of showing this Paper before it was Publish'd to a judicious and learned Friend, a Man indefatigably zealous in the service of the Church and State" (I, 302-3). As his refusal to remove an offensive opinion from the poem indicates, however, he was even more determined to state what as a "layman" he honestly believed: "No man's Faith depends upon his will," he declares in the poem; "*MY* Salvation must its Doom receive/Not from what *OTHERS*, but what *I* believe" (ll. 442, 302-3).

Religio Laici is not then an apology for the Anglican faith; it employs the "already Consecrated" works of the Church not as the materials of Dryden's own confession but as "Weapons . . . employed for the common Cause, against the Enemies of Piety" (I, 302). His own faith rests *entirely* upon the revelation of "Heaven's Will" in those parts of Scripture which are necessary to his salvation and which, according to his understanding, are "clear" and "sufficient" (l. 167) to this end. It is a sceptic's faith, not imposed upon others because not demonstrably verifiable—indeed, embraced by Dryden *because* man's limited access to certainty is not called upon. *Religio Laici* accordingly begins with an expression of Dryden's sceptical view of the limited value of human reason in spiritual matters:

> Dim, as the borrow'd beams of Moon and Stars
> To *lonely, weary, wandring* Travellers,
> Is *Reason* to the *Soul:* and as on high,
> Those rowling Fires *discover* but the Sky
> Not light us *here;* So *Reason's* glimmering Ray

> Was lent, not to *assure* our *doubtfull* way,
> But *guide* us upward to a *better Day.*
> And as those nightly Tapers disappear
> When Day's bright Lord ascends our Hemisphere;
> So pale grows *Reason* at *Religions* sight:
> So *dyes,* and so *dissolves* in *Supernatural Light.* (11. 1-11)

These opening lines of the poem consist of three distinct but connected similes comparing the relative value to travelers of the heavenly lights of night and day with the relative value to the soul of the natural light of reason and the supernatural light of religion: (1) as the borrowed light of moon and stars is dim to lonely, weary, wandering travelers, so is reason dim to the soul; (2) as those rolling fires discover but the sky, not light us here, so reason's glimmering ray was lent to guide us upward to a better day, not to assure our doubtful way; (3) as those nightly tapers disappear when day's bright lord ascends our hemisphere, so reason grows pale, dies, and dissolves in supernatural light at the sight of religion. At only one point in these three equations is the analogy not at once apparent, and this is the only point in the passage which indicates the value of reason; in what way then, one must ask, is the function of the heavenly bodies to "discover but the sky" analogous to the function of reason "to guide us upward to a better day?"

Dryden says that as illumination of the *path* or "way" which the traveler must follow, the light of the moon and stars is worthless; it does "not light us here." Only the light of the sun illuminates the path. The light of the moon and stars reveals nothing but the trackless black of the sky. Like a "taper," this light draws the eye of the traveler *from* his path *to* the sky, where, as the only light in the dark, its mere visibility offers the promise of daylight. This is its only value. The value of reason to the soul is similarly limited. The natural light of reason provides no illumination for the soul; it does not make safe ("assure") its spiritual course. Only a "a better day" (the "supernatural light" of religion) can illuminate the way of the soul. Like the light of the stars ("those rowling fires"), the light of reason reveals only its own inadequacy in spiritual matters, guiding—again as the stars do—not by illuminating the way but by directing the gaze "upward" to heaven. (Dryden again used this image in the poem to indicate the moral confusion of rational attempts to find the *Summum Bonum*: "Thus, *anxious Thoughts* in *endless Circles* roul,/Without a *Centre* where to fix the *Soul*" [11. 36-37]). Fujimura believes Dryden's lines mean that "without revelation . . . we must stumble along by the light of natural reason";[14] read objectively, however, they more definitely indicate that reason will not serve in even this capacity; its value as a "guide" to the soul is to reveal its own limitations, *thereby* directing the soul to the light of religion or revelation.

Dryden's scepticism of the cognitive value of human reason in spiritual matters is the keynote of the entire poem; restated throughout in countless images of light and sight, it is the reference for his attack upon the rational presumption of the Deists (11. 42-98), his defense of revelation (11. 99-167), and his criticism of the dogmatism of the Catholics (11. 276-397) and of the Sectarians (11. 398-426). Given to us as the means of recognizing only the obvious truth that "*finite Reason*" cannot reach Infinity (1. 40) and, or course, as the means of reading "*Heaven's Will*" in Scripture, reason is described in the first half of the poem as inadequate and as a source of error. Even the ancient heathen, "those Gyant Wits," were unable to answer "the great ends of humane kind," the knowledge of "how *God* may be *appeas'd,* and *Mortals blest*" (11. 131-33). Dryden argues (and in this, he departs from Anglican doctrine) that the heathen belief in one God was not a natural discovery of reason but a racial inheritance of the revelation made in Noah's time (Preface, I, 303); and those "few" who, by reason, were led to a conception of one God, were, it must be inferred, using the light of Nature merely to reclaim that revealed truth which men "in the Posterity of *Noah*" had forgotten. The truths of natural religion propounded by the Deist (the belief that there is one God, that prayer and praise are his due worship) are similarly, he believes, "the remote effects of Revelation" (Preface, I, 304):

> These Truths are not the product of thy Mind,
> But dropt from Heaven, and of a Nobler kind.
> *Reveal'd Religion* first inform'd thy Sight,
> And *Reason* saw not, till *Faith* sprung the Light.
> Hence all thy *Natural Worship* takes the *Source:*
> 'Tis *Revelation* what thou thinkst *Discourse.* (11. 65-70)

Even when these revealed truths provide the foundation for a rationally devised religion, the result is self-defeating, encouraging not moral goodness, but cruelty and sin. Thus the ancients attempted to expiate their sins by bribing God with the sacrifice of the "guiltless": "Ah! at how cheap a rate the *Rich* might Sin!" (1. 90). The natural light of reason appeals always to natural interests; it indulges our "Sense" and is fed "by Natures Soil, in which it grows" (11. 157-60). The less barbarous Deist substitutes remorse for sacrifice, but he underestimates the gravity of his sin and consults his own comfort in exacting the penalty he shall pay for it. Even if he were objective in this respect, however, his debt could not be paid; for, since man's sin "is made against *Omnipotence*,/Some Price, that bears *proportion*, must be paid;/And *Infinite* with *Infinite* be weigh'd":

> See then the *Deist lost: Remorse* for *Vice*,
> *Not* paid, or *paid, inadequate* in price:
> What farther means can *Reason* now direct,
> Or what Relief from *humane Wit* expect?
> *That* shews us sick; and sadly are we sure
> *Still* to be *Sick*, till *Heav'n* reveal the *Cure*. (11. 113-20)

Heaven's "cure" is, of course, the record of God's "*Will reveal'd*" in Scripture; and Dryden is able to accept its validity precisely because its law transcends nature and, therefore, appeals not to man's "interest" but to his "Charity." Yet, though he says "proof needs not here" (1. 126), he is required to defend the validity of revelation against the objections of the Deists and the dogmatism of the Catholics, and to distinguish between his "layman's liberty" in reading the Scriptures and the "private spirit" of the Puritans. His answer to the Deist's objection to the validity of supernatural law is especially interesting inasmuch as it differentiates between his private faith and his Anglican defense of that faith. The Deist argues that if "a *general Law* is that alone/Which must to *all*, and every *where* be known," then how can the law of Scripture (which cannot claim "a Style so large") be considered sufficient? (11. 168-73). More than any other, Dryden admits, this argument can "startle Reason, stagger frail Belief" (11. 184-85)—i.e., if not undermine the supernatural basis of religion, at least *arouse* reason to its defense,[15] which as Athanasius' condemnation of the heathen illustrates, is much the same thing. Dryden feels free to reject Athanasius' view as a form of rational dogmatism which in addition is untrue to the merciful spirit of Christian law:

'Tis hard for *Man* to doom to *endless pains*
All who believ'd not all, his Zeal requir'd:
Unless he first cou'd prove he was inspir'd. (11. 215-17)

The Athanasian condemnation may be only the *zealotry* of a mere "*Man*," one who, "unless . . . inspir'd," was "too eager in dispute," and thus "Flew high" (11. 221-22). Dryden's belief, though simple, is not "frail"; he identifies himself with those who have faith alone in the "*boundless Wisedom*" and "*boundless Mercy*" of God; and, having faith, he invokes not reason or interest but charity to answer the Deist:

Nor does it baulk my *Charity*, to find
Th' *Egyptian* Bishop [Athanasius] of another mind. (11. 212-13)

If from his [God's] *Nature Foes* may Pity claim,
Much more may *Strangers* who ne'er heard his *Name*.
And though *no Name* be for Salvation known,
But that of his *Eternal Sons* alone;
Who knows how far transcending Goodness can
Extend the *Merits* of *that Son* to *Man*? (11. 190-95)

The question of the possibility of salvation without revelation is, for Dryden, academic; as far as he himself is concerned, the means of salvation have been revealed in terms about which there can be no misunderstanding. But to answer the Deist's objection he must go further than this: "Not only *Charity* bids hope the *best*,/But *more* the great Apostle has exprest" (11. 198-99). What follows is Paul's justification of the Gentiles by natural reason, a "righteous Doom," according to Dryden (since "a Rule *reveal'd*/Is *none* to *Those*, from whom it was *conceal'd* [11. 206-7]), but one which human reason cannot reconcile with the traditional Christian belief that salvation is only possible through faith in God as revealed in Christ, the Word. Dryden therefore distinguishes Paul's view as something "more" than his own simple faith, something greater than what he is capable of understanding, since as a man of mere reason he can believe it as a truth only by the authority of the Apostle.

Humbly recognizing his "little Skill," Dryden is always prepared to *submit* his opinion to his "Mother-Church" (11. 318-19); at the same time, he assumes "an honest *Layman's Liberty*" (1. 317), for "the things we *must* believe, are *few*, and *plain*" (1. 432); and "'Tis some Relief, that points not clearly known/Without much hazard may be let alone" (11. 444-45). There are "plain *Truths* enough for needful *use*" (1. 409), Dryden believes, and on these alone rest his faith—not merely because this is also the counsel of his Church but because, in his sceptical way, he can accept only these truths. Beyond this, he will proceed only tentatively, following the charitable spirit of his faith as the most disinterested and therefore most trustworthy guide. In the second half of *Religio Laici*, Dryden defends this faith against the two enemies who would deprive him of this source of spiritual guidance: the Catholics who, "under the pretence of Infalibility," invest the Church with the exclusive right of Scriptural interpretation; and the Sectaries or "Fanaticks," who assume individually "what amounts to an Infalibility, in the private Spirit," and in so doing "have detorted those Texts of Scripture, which are not necessary to Salvation, to the damnable uses of Sedition" (Preface, I, 306).

It is significant that although Dryden as an Anglican attacks the Sectaries for their stiffnecked reliance upon the private spirit, as a sceptic he condemns them for forming with the Catholics a united front of dogmatism, since both claim to be infallible. "What then remains," Dryden writes, "but, waving each Extreme,/The tides of Ignorance, and Pride to stem" (11. 427-28). Chiasson, who argues that Dryden here continues to combat the Puritan private spirit with Anglican reason, says that "Dryden is anxious to 'stem' both the 'tides of ignorance' (Puritans) and 'pride' (Roman Catholics)."[16] Clearly, however, Dryden means that it is the Catholic Church which has condemned its communicants to ignorance in making them "so rich a Treasure [the Scriptures] to forgo" (1. 429), and the Puritans who "proudly seek beyond [their] pow'r to know" (1. 430). In taking up Goliath's Sword of Anglican polemics "for the common Cause," Dryden has not betrayed his private cause of scepticism in its battle against dogmatism.

After stating his personal faith in the possible salvation of the heathen, Dryden writes that "thus far" his "crude thoughts" were "bred" by reading Father Simon's *Critical History* (11. 224-28), a work which repudiated the sufficiency of Scripture unsupplemented by Roman Catholic tradition. Paradoxically, Dryden's reading of Father Simon's criticism of Scriptural authority weakened the argument for the infallibility of the Church; indeed, he implies that Simon's real intention in the *History* may be precisely what Dryden makes of the work—an argument against all dogmatism: "For some, who have his secret meaning ghes'd, /Have found our Authour not too *much* a *Priest*" (11. 252-53).[17] From Simon's thesis, Dryden argues that "if *God's own People*, who of God before/Knew what we know . . . and who did neither *Time*, nor *Study* spare/To keep this Book *untainted, unperplext*;/Let in gross *Errours* to corrupt the *Text*," then even less certainty can be expected from commentators still further removed from the original writers of Scripture (11. 260-69). To be sure, tradition—and, in particular, written tradition—is not "useless . . . when general, old, disinteress'd and clear" (11. 334-35); the earliest traditions would in fact constitute "proof . . . cou'd we be *certain*" they were "*first Traditions*" (11. 342-43). But in view of human fallibility, such certainty cannot be assumed; at best, tradition constitutes only "probability" which serves merely to "confirm" what may be already accepted as self-evident truth.

Thus Dryden uses the *Critical History* to support his sceptical rejection of dogmatism and to justify his humble reliance upon those few texts "sufficient, clear, intire,/In *all* things which our needful *Faith* require" (11. 299-300). Since the Church can offer no proof of the authenticity of the texts it interprets, there can be no "*unerring Guid*" outside of Scripture itself: "*God wou'd not leave Mankind without a way:*/ And that the *Scriptures* . . ." (11. 295-96). In this "Safe" and "modest" conclusion Dryden attempts to reconcile his sceptical faith with his professed Anglicanism.

II *Roman Catholic Fideism and* The Hind and the Panther

Five years after the publication of *Religio Laici*, Dryden penned the following confession near the beginning of his poetic apology of Roman Catholicism, *The Hind and the Panther*:

> . . . . gratious God, how well dost thou provide
> For erring judgments an unerring Guide?
> Thy throne is darkness in th' abyss of light,
> A blaze of glory that forbids the sight;
> O teach me to believe Thee thus conceal'd,
> And search no farther than thy self reveal'd;
> But her alone for my Directour take,

> Whom thou hast promis'd never to forsake!
> My thoughtless youth was wing'd with vain desires,
> My manhood, long misled by wandring fires,
> Follow'd false lights; and when their glimps was gone,
> My pride struck out new sparkles of her own.
> Such was I, such by nature still I am,
> Be thine the glory, and be mine the shame. (11. 64-77)

By a development of the light-sight imagery with which he had expressed the superiority of revelation to reason in *Religio Laici,* Dryden may suggest here the change in point of view which led to his conversion to Catholicism. Here again are the misleading "wandring fires"—the "rowling fires" of the earlier poem—symbolizing the rational approach to religion which antedated his profession of faith in *Religio Laici.* But, he now maintains, even when the attractions of reason had been subdued, his "pride struck out new sparkles of her own." That "honest layman's liberty" which reserved the right to accept only those parts of Scripture which, by virtue of their plainness, he deemed necessary for his salvation is repudiated here as a form of presumption, as is also his expedient of tentative assent to the probability of those parts of Scripture which were deemed "unnecessary" for his own salvation: "To take up half on trust, and half to try,/Name it not faith, but bungling biggottry" (Pt. 1, 11. 141-42), he now writes in *The Hind and the Panther.* Dryden views the independent faith expressed in *Religio Laici* as little better than that prompted by the private spirit of the extreme Protestant sects; for, without an infallible authority to which Scriptural interpretation may be referred, the individual must resort to "conscience," merely another name "with man below" for "interest" (Pt. 3, 11. 823-24).

Dryden's altered view of the Anglican Church, symbolized in the poem by the Panther, is a masterly achievement of objective statement. In terms of the beast fable, she is the creature second only to the Hind (the Catholic Church) in nobility, beauty, and goodness; nevertheless, she is "a beast of Prey" (sired by the adulterous lion Henry VIII), her external spots betraying "her inborn stains":

> How can I praise, or blame, and not offend,
> Or how divide the frailty from the friend!
> Her faults and vertues lye so mix'd, that she
> Nor wholly stands condemn'd, nor wholly free. (Pt. 1, 11. 331-34)

Dryden solves this problem in the second and third parts of the poem through the use of the dramatic debate, the literary form toward which his sceptical temperament naturally disposed him, and which here permitted the Panther to betray her own faults while the peaceloving Hind revealed her virtues in the effort to conciliate their differences. In Part 1—the style of which, Dryden notes in his prefatory "To the Reader," is raised and given "the Majestick Turn of Heroick Poesie" (II, 469)—the delineation of the Panther's character and the survey of her history follows the introduction of the Hind and "the *wolfish* crew" of English Sectaries, as well as the narrator's statement of his position with respect to the value of reason, sense, and faith as guides in religious matters. The organization thus clearly distinguishes the moderate position of the Anglican Church from the extremist sects, but also, in revealing its differences from the Catholic Church, points up the responsibility of Anglicanism in fostering those sects.

The weakness of the Anglican Church, Dryden implies, lies in its moderation; for, while it accepts the central mysteries of Christianity as a matter of faith beyond the reach of human reason, it makes no claim to infallibility in their interpretation. And, in order to defend its differences with the Catholic Church and the English sects, it must appeal either to the "private conscience" or to the senses. The Anglican has thus rejected the Catholic doctrine of transubstantiation because the senses deny that one body can occupy more than one place at a time (Pt. 1, 11. 100-5), a view which Dryden finds even less defensible than the rationalist's approach to religion: "Can I my reason to my faith compell,/And shall my sight, and touch, and taste rebell?" (11. 85-86). Nor is the Anglican any better able to reconcile the contradictory interpretations of the Eucharist among the sects—"where one for substance, one for sign contends": "Her Novices are taught that bread and wine/Are but the visible and outward sign. . . . His bloud and body, who to save us dy'd;/The faithful this thing signify'd receive. . . . They take the sign, and take the substance too." Dryden wryly comments on such a view by saying that, although "the lit'ral sense" of the mystery of the Eucharist is "hard to flesh and blood," "nonsense never can be understood" (11. 411-29). When such "winding ways" fail to resolve doubts, the Panther "slips herself aside/And leaves the private conscience for the guide" (11. 476-78). She is, therefore, neither loved nor feared; she is "a mere mock Queen of a divided Herd" (11. 497-98), over whom her authority will be "lawful" only when she herself recognizes the infallibility of the true queen of the forest, the Hind:

> Then, as the Moon who first receives the light
> By which she makes our nether regions bright,
> So might she shine, reflecting from afar
> The rays she borrow'd from a better star:
> Big with the beams which from her mother flow
> And reigning o'er the rising tides below. (11. 501-6)

That "better star," by whose influence the moon may control the "tides" of Protestant individualism is, of course, the Roman Church, "Heav'n's authority," the "Eternal house, not built with mortal hands" (Pt. 1, 1. 494). The infallibility of its doctrine resides in the decree of the "Pope and gen'ral councils . . . both combin'd" (Pt. 2, 11. 81-82), "assisted from above with God's unfailing grace" (Pt. 2, 1. 95). In opposition to the Anglican license of individual interpretation of "needful" points— in effect a "pretense/To plead the Scriptures in their own defense" (11. 154-55)—the Catholic has recourse to the corporate reason of the Church, which derives "from sire to son" by the force of a tradition extending back to Christ's ministry, no age trusting further "than the next above" (11. 216-19). Since no written law can be so plain "but wit may gloss, and malice may obscure," faith was planted by tradition before the written word appeared "and men believ'd, not what they read, but heard" (11. 318-23). Tradition must therefore be the test of Scripture—not, as the Anglican would have it, the other way around. The Anglican, since he himself interprets the sense of Scripture, merely replaces an informed authority with an uninformed authority.

"About a Fortnight" before he finished *The Hind and the Panther*, Dryden writes in his prefatory "To the Reader," James II issued his "Declaration of Conscience," granting freedom of worship to all dissenters from the Anglican Church and suspending all penal laws and the Test Act, hitherto a prerequisite for public officeholders. Had he anticipated this policy, Dryden continues, "I might have spar'd my self the labour of writing many things which are contain'd in the third part [of the poem]. But I was alwayes in some hope, that the Church of *England* might have been perswaded to have taken off the *Penal Lawes* and the *Test,* which was one Design of the Poem when I propos'd to my self the writing of it" (II, 468). Accordingly, in the third part of the poem, the Hind has fearlessly ("because the *Lyon's* peace was now proclaim'd" [1. 21]) offered the Panther the shelter of her "lowly roof" for the night:

> The wary salvage would not give offence,
> To forfeit the protection of her *Prince;*
> But watch'd the time her vengeance to compleat. (11. 22-24)

It is clear, however, that the toleration achieved by James' declaration was not that for which Dryden hoped at the outset of the poem. At the beginning of his reign, the new king attempted to ally the Anglicans and Catholics against the Dissenters, a policy which Dryden appears to endorse throughout the first two parts of the poem. When, however, Parliament refused to repeal those laws which were prejudicial to the Catholics, James employed his royal prerogative to secure a general dispensation which included the Dissenters. Unprepared for such a move, Dryden apparently tried (though not with complete consistency) to bring the poem into line with this policy. The harsh treatment of the Dissenters in the first two parts of the poem is somewhat softened in the Preface by a compromising statement on conscience, and the satire of the third part of the poem is more carefully aimed at the Panther, the "least deform'd" of the beasts. The familiarity assured by the *"Lyon's* peace" enables the Hind to discover a new "malady" in the mind of the Panther:

> Disdain, with gnawing envy, fell despight,
> And canker'd malice stood in open sight.
> Ambition, int'rest, pride without controul,
> And jealousie, the jaundice of the soul;
> Revenge, the bloudy minister of ill,
> With all the lean tormenters of the will. (11. 70-75)

In fact, Dryden believes that the precipitancy of James' declaration may have endangered the cause of Catholicism in England. Conversion is not a "profitable change," the Hind remarks (1. 363); Dryden himself, she implies, pays "small attendance at the *Lyon's* court" (1. 236). Anglican jealousy is unjustified, for the Catholic's peace will probably end with James' successor: the "respite" they enjoy is "onely lent./The best they have to hope, protracted punishment" (11. 380-83).

The first of the "two *Episodes,* or *Fables,*" which are "interwoven with the main Design" (II, 469) of the third part of the poem indicates that Dryden, along with the more moderate English Catholics, disapproved of the aggressive policies of James' Jesuit confessor Father Petre. Related by the Panther as a "timely warning" to the Hind and to her sons against "eager haste and gaudy hopes and giddy pride" (1. 424), the fable of the swallows emphasizes the need for foresight in gauging the "changes of winds" on which the welfare of religion depends. Fearful of migration and foolishly trusting in the clemency of the winter (James' reign), the swallows (English Catholics) are encouraged by a cowardly and superstitious martin (Father Petre) to postpone a trip to warmer climes. Confident that some unexpected signs of spring predict that "for their sakes, the sun shou'd backward go" (1. 534), the swallows "repossess their patrimonial sky"; but they are soon overwhelmed by a north wind (the Protestant reign likely to follow James') which "powr'd amain/His ratling hail-stones mix'd with snow and rain":

> The joyless morning late arose, and found
> A dreadful desolation reign a-round,
> Some buried in the Snow, some frozen to the ground:
>
> . . . .
>
> *Martyn* himself was caught a-live, and try'd
> For treas'nous crimes, because the laws provide
> No *Martyn* there in winter shall abide. (11. 620-34).

Although Dryden appears to have regarded the king's pro-Catholic measures as rash, it is felt by most scholars that he puts the blame not upon James but upon Father Petre. But, if so, it does not seem likely that Dryden implies that the swallows should reject the martin's advice, that English Catholics should seek refuge abroad. The Panther admits that the martin is not "blameless" (1. 653); yet even more "she mark'd the malice" of the Panther's tale as it applied to his "character" (1. 640). The fable then is more than a caveat for James' Jesuit advisors; it is, first of all, a satiric exposure by the Hind of "the *Panther's* hate,/The people's rage, the persecuting State" (1. 645-46). In the lines which follow, the Panther, while protesting her loyalty to the king, reveals that her opposition to James' Declaration of Indulgence is based upon self-interest, and thus she betrays her own weakness. "Your care about your Banks, infers a fear/Of threat'ning Floods," the Hind explains:

> If so, a just Reprise would only be
> Of what the Land usurp'd upon the Sea;
> And all your Jealousies but serve to show
> Your Ground is, like your Neighbour-Nation, low.
> T' intrench in what you grant unrighteous Laws
> Is to distrust the justice of your Cause;
> And argues that the true Religion lyes
> In those weak Adversaries you despise. (11. 860-69)

Dryden thus appears to consider the Anglican fear of a Catholic colony in England and the Anglicans' reason for opposing repeal of the Test Act even more immoderate than the king's disregard of the probable consequences of his action. As the Hind reminds the Panther, there may be another consequence to this state of affairs, one, she suggests, which may be more "unlucky" for the Anglicans than for the Catholics (11. 649-50). Reprisal from the Lion, the Panther need not, of course, fear (1. 870); the Hind only hopes that the Panther's new alliance with the wolf (the Presbyterian) will "more successful prove,/Than was the *Pigeons* and the *Buzzards* love" (11. 898-99), whose story, as an opposing parallel to the Panther's fable she, in turn, relates.

The Hind's fable serves to balance and to allay English Catholic fear (the alternative to Jesuit zeal in the Panther's fable) by revealing the folly and danger of Anglican fears of James' policies. The Catholics ("Domestick Poultry"), not the Anglicans (pigeons), are the rightful residents of the farmyard in this tale; the latter, though "voracious Birds, that hotly Bill and breed" (1. 950), are nevertheless well served by the "Plain good' farmer (James): "bound by Promise, he supports their Cause,/As Corporations privileg'd by Laws" (11. 953-54). Yet the pigeons' greed (Anglican interest) makes peace impossible: "when some Lay-preferment fell by chance/The Gourmands made it their Inheritance" (11. 968-69); and, envious of the chickens' holy habits ("midnight Mattins, at uncivil Hours"

[1. 1010]), the pigeons embarked upon a program of vilification:

An hideous Figure of their Foes they drew,
Nor Lines, nor Looks, nor Shades, nor Colours true;
And this Grotesque design, expos'd to Publick view. (11. 1042-44)

Indeed, the pigeons decreed (11. 1078-79) that "none to Trust, or Profit should succeed,/Who would not swallow first a poysonous wicked Weed" (the Test Act), and when the farmer tried by "gentle means" to remove "th' Effects of so unnatural a Law" (11. 1085-86), they employed the buzzard (the anti-Catholic and onetime Presbyterian Gilbert Burnet) to cuff "the tender *Chickens* from their food" (1. 1224). At this, the farmer "pronounc'd a Doom/Of Sacred Strength" making "all Birds of ev'ry Sect/Free of his Farm, with promise to respect/Their sev'ral Kinds alike, and equally protect" (11. 1244-46). All this the Panther might well be expected to know; "what after happen'd," though "not hard to guess," constitutes the Hind's warning to her. Repenting "too late," the pigeons "become the Smiths of their own Foolish Fate" (11. 1267-68); the buzzard, now prohibited from enjoying his favorite food, chicken, "may be tempted to his former fare," pigeon (1. 1281). The latter, "Rent in Schism, (for so their Fate decrees,)" will be an easy prey, the Hind warns: "They fight their Quarrel, by themselves opprest,/The Tyrant smiles below, and waits the falling feast" (11. 1285-88).

Although Dryden believed that the fables of Aesop and Spenser provided adequate precedent in the use of the beast fable (Pt. 3, 11. 6-15), few modern critics have been able to overlook the incongruity implicit in animals which engage in theological argument; and in Dryden's own day, Charles Montague and Matthew Prior burlesqued the idea in their *Story of the City and Country Mouse.* Dryden, however, apparently felt justified in the choice of the form, for "If men transact like brutes 'tis equal then/For brutes to claim the privilege of men" (Pt. 3, 11. 14-15). "Beasts are the subjects of tyrannick sway,/Where still the stronger on the weaker prey" (Pt. 1, 11. 245-46): man alone was made "not for his fellows ruine, but their aid" (1. 248), and he was therefore endowed with mercy as his distinguishing attribute. But in the world of religious persecution (the worst of "the tyrannies on humane kind"), man has overthrown "the laws of nations and of nature too" (1. 244). Protestant dogmatism, Dryden is suggesting, has metamorphosed its adherents into hunters and beasts of prey, into men who have deserted Christ ("Pan"), the protector of sheep and the "harmless Hind" (11. 284-86). Thus the Catholic *Hind and the Panther* reveals its essential consistency not only with Dryden's fideist appeal to charity in *Religio Laici*, but with his conservative defense of monarchy in *Absalom and Achitophel* and in *The Medall*.

CHAPTER 7

Late Lyrics and Translations

Dryden was extraordinarily productive in his last fifteen years; near the very end of his life he could remark in the Preface to *The Fables*: thoughts "come crowding in so fast upon me, that my only Difficulty is to chuse or to reject; to run them into Verse, or to give them the other Harmony of Prose."[1] Although a large part of the work of these years consists of translation, it is not to be thought that this emphasis indicates a drying up of the springs of creativity; translation was not for Dryden a subordinate labor, less demanding upon the wit and judgment of the poet than original creation. Moreover, his work with the Classics—just as, from the beginning, his original work—eventuated in some of his most interesting critical writing: the long "Discourse concerning the Original and Progress of Satire," for instance, or the Dedication of the *Aeneid,* and of course the splendid Preface to *The Fables.*

Most surprising is the continuance of his lyrical powers in these later years, particularly at the lofty altitude of the Pindaric ode. Mark Van Doren has remarked that Dryden was "constitutionally adapted to a form of exalted utterance which progressed by the alternate accumulating and discharging of metrical energy," a characteristic earlier exemplified by the "swells in the stream of his heroic verse";[2] note should also be taken of the less elevated lyrics in the songs and dances included in many of his plays, of his interest in opera and, later, in the masque, and, for that matter, of the appeal to the ear made by his verse of every kind. In the last respect, the use (perhaps overuse) of the Alexandrine and the triplet comes most readily to mind; but more generally, he knew, as Dr. Johnson said, "how to choose the flowing and the sonorous words, to vary the pauses and adjust the accents, to diversify the cadence, and yet preserve the smoothness of his metre."[3]

I *Pindaric Odes*

Dryden very likely had mixed feelings about the Pindaric ode. In view of his lifelong dedication to the heroic mode in poetry, it is to be expected that he should essay the form which shared the Neoclassical category of "greater Poetry" with the epic and tragedy. Cowley's "translations" from Pindar in 1656 quickly established it—in distinction to the "little" Horatian ode—as the form which allowed "more Latitude than any other," and thus the proper vehicle for great subjects. But Dryden was also dedicated to "Nature" and to decorum in art, and the "Pindarick" was a license to abandon art to enthusiasm, and to permit subject matter to carry the poet, unhampered by stanza form, line length, and rhyme scheme, wherever it might. As such, it becomes the most abused form in English poetry, and by 1711 called forth Addison's ridicule of the poet who follows "Irregularities by Rule."[4] It is not surprising, therefore, that Dryden approached the Pindaric ode with cautious moderation. Its popularity, he recognized, was due to its "seeming easiness": yet Pindar is "difficult" to imitate; Cowley's odes are marked by "Warmth and Vigor of Fancy . . . masterly Figures, and the copiousness of Imagination": yet they want "Purity of *English*, somewhat of more equal of Thoughts . . . of sweetness in the Numbers, in one Word, somewhat of a finer turn and more Lyrical Verse."[5]

Dryden's first attempt at the form, a rendering into "pindaricks" of the twenty-ninth ode of the third book of Horace, is thus not only a liberating of Horatian correctness but a refining of Pindaric vigor. The Preface to *Sylvae*, in which volume this ode appeared, defines his practice:

> Since *Pindar* was the Prince of *Lyrick* Poets; let me have leave to say, that, in imitating him, our numbers shou'd, for the most part be Lyrical: For variety, or rather where the Majesty of the thought requires it, they may be stretch'd to the *English* Heroick of five Feet, and to the *French* Alexandrine of Six. But the ear must preside, and direct the Judgment to the choice of numbers . . . the cadency of one line must be a rule to that of the next; and the sound of the former must slide gently into that which follows; without leaping from one extream into another. (I, 400)

Dryden's poem is closer to the spirit than to the carefully

patterned form of the authentic Pindaric ode. His amplifica-
tion to 104 lines of Horace's sixty-four, is grouped into ten
stanzas ranging in length from four to seventeen lines. Metrically
less spectacular than Cowley's efforts, Dryden reserves his
repertory of special effects for passages of natural description,
of which the seventh stanza is the most ambitious:

> Enjoy the present smiling hour;
> And put it out of Fortune's pow'r:
> The tide of bus'ness, like the running stream,
> Is sometimes high, and sometimes low,
> A quiet ebb, or a tempestuous flow,
> And alwayes in extream.
> Now with a noiseless gentle course
> It keeps within the middle Bed:
> Anon it lifts aloft the head,
> And bears down all before it, with impetuous force:
> And trunks of Trees come rowling down,
> Sheep and their Folds together drown:
> Both House and Homestead into Seas are borne,
> And Rocks are from their old foundations torn,
> And woods made thin with winds, their scatter'd honours mourn.
>
> (11. 50-64)

The most striking effect here is of course onomatopoetic, the
acceleration of the pace in the second half of the stanza to
accompany the reference to the "running stream" of a life
of business; and, in the first half, the metrical extremity of
shifting from five feet to three in the foreshortened sixth line
to articulate the *extremes* of Fortune in that life. Of more
significance for the lyricism of the passage is the harmonizing
of this metrical variety through the subtle shading of "*o*" sounds
in such words as "hour," "out," "pow'r," and "now," "Fortune's,"
"low," "flow," and "course," and in "anon," "aloft," "Rocks," and
"from." "It must be done," Dryden explained in his Preface, "like
the shadowings of a Picture, which fall by degrees into a
darker colour" (I, 400).

Two more Pindaric odes appeared in 1685: *Threnodia Augustalis*—an ode on the death of Charles II—and the memorial
piece to Anne Killigrew. The *Threnodia* was an official duty
of Charles' "servant"; but, since Dryden evidently expected
to maintain his place as Laureate under the successor, he
produced at once an elegy for Charles II and an encomium

to James II, a decision which further recommended the "latitude" of the Pindaric. The ambitious design of eighteen stanzas, ranging in length from twelve to forty-two lines, was determined, therefore, less by lyrical impetuosity than by the political necessity of its double theme: "The King is dead! Long live the King!" Dryden wished to strengthen the stability of the Stuart dynasty in the reign of the Catholic James; he had, therefore, to address the poem not only to "the present Age," which owed Charles its "Pious Praise" for securing the English subjects' freedom, but to "Posterity"—to James' subjects:

Posterity is charg'd the more,
Because the large abounding store
To them and to their Heirs, is still entail'd by thee.
Succession, of a long Descent

. . . .
Thou hast deriv'd this mighty Blessing down,
And fixt the fairest Gemm that decks th' Imperial Crown.
    (11. 308-17)

This greater debt to Charles can be paid only by the subjects' loyalty to James, whose grief and whose strength at Charles' death are depicted as both the example and justification of true allegiance.

Threnodia Augustalis may be divided into three parts, the stanzaic order throughout roughly following a chronological sequence. The first part deals with events leading up to Charles' death: the unexpected news of the king's illness and the sudden onslaught of grief in the poet and the public (stanza i), and in James (stanza ii); Charles' rally (stanza iii), and the effects of mixed hope and fear for the outcome (stanza iv); the physician's heroic battle against "th' impregnable Disease" (stanza v), and Charles' even more heroic acceptance of "the griesly Challenger," Death (stanza vi). The death of the king is viewed here as the disruption of order in man and nature, a Lucretian holocaust (11. 31-33). The nation's grief is defined in terms of climatic upheaval ("Hurricane") and, since "arbitrary" and "unbounded by a Law" (1. 62), political anarchy. The passions of hope and fear are tyrannical, making "well meaning . . . Petitioners" (1. 100) of their subjects, whose prayers for Charles' recovery resemble the Cyclops' rebellion against Heaven's will (11. 103-4). Even James, the Hercules who will maintain order, "first was seen to fear," and "half unarray'd . . . ran to his

Relief" (11. 53-54). Charles' acceptance of death is the first step towards the restoration of order; the calm dignity and metrical regularity of the sixth stanza are thus a fitting prelude to James' emergence as the new king in the third part of the ode.

The transitional second part is formally elegiac in nature, consisting chiefly of a catalog of Charles' blessings. It begins properly (stanza vii) with the king's bequest of "all that on earth he held most dear" to him whose right was given by "both heav'n . . . and his own Love" (11. 224-28). There follow a tribute to his "all forgiving" mind, (stanza viii); a description of his death (stanza ix); the list of his gifts to the nation (stanzas x-xiii), the greatest of which being the perpetuation of the principle of hereditary monarchy according to law; and finally (stanza xiv) the formal elegiac questioning of Providence, which is resolved in the last lines of the section: "The chosen Flock has now the Promis'd Land [the New Canaan-England under James] in view" (1. 428). Charles' greatest blessing is thus identified with his successor; and, from this point to the end, the poem's emphasis shifts to James, "a Warlike Prince" (1. 429), and the hero best equipped to maintain that blessing. The reference, in the opening stanza of the ode, to Hercules' taking the weight of the world from Atlas is thus an anticipation of the development of James as the hero. Like his prototype, James too was hardened by adversity in his youth, having had to grapple with Juno's twin snakes ("his Father's Rebels, and his Brother's Foes" [1. 460]). He is, therefore, prepared to undertake the labors of his fate both at home (in subduing "the *Hydra* of the many-headed, hissing Crew" [1. 464]) and abroad (stanza xvii). This third section of the ode is disappointing, however; and, though the welcome of the new king is structurally well conceived, its execution is perfunctory.

In the ode to Anne Killigrew, Dryden is entirely successful. Here the motives of elegy and ode—grief for the daughter of an old acquaintence, and praise of her accomplishments as a poet and painter—are combined in the Renaissance conception of the artist. The formal parts of the elegy[6]—the apostrophe to (stanza i) and praise of the dead person (stanzas ii, iii); the lament for the times (stanza iv) which, in combination with the listing of the dead person's virtues (stanzas v-vii), leads

to the questioning of Providence (stanza viii); the grief of the
mourners (Anne's seafaring brother) (stanza ix); and the consolation (stanza x)—are here adapted, in terms of Anne's accomplishments as an artist, to the form and purpose of the ode:
to the degree that earthly poetry partakes of the divine, the
lament for her death is also a paean of her victory. Thus by
virtue of her earthly poems (which made her a "Probationer,
and Candidate of Heav'n"), Anne has become "a welcome In-
mate there" (stanza i); and Dryden may speculate upon whether
her poetic soul was derived by natural "Traduction" (inheritance
from her father) or by transmigration from Sappho, having
moved through "all the Mighty Poets" until it resided in a
suitably refined body, thence to "return, to fill or mend the
Quire, of thy Celestial kind" (stanza ii). So, too, in the consoling
vision of "the last Assizes" with which the poem ends, it
is "the Sacred Poets" who first shall hear the trumpet of
Judgment:

> And formost from the Tomb shall bound:
> For they are cover'd with the lightest Ground
> And streight, with in-born Vigour, on the Wing,
> Like mounting Larkes, to the New Morning sing.
> There *Thou*, Sweet Saint, before the Quire shalt go,
> As Harbinger of Heav'n, the Way to show,
> The Way which thou so well hast learn'd below. (11. 189-95)

The priority extended to the poets here is a reflection of
the Classical conception of art as order, an idealized image
of nature reflected or "design'd" by the artist's soul (11. 106-7).
Thus, although "cold herself," Anne's love poetry "such Warmth
exprest,/'Twas *Cupid* bathing in Diana's Stream" (11. 83-87).
Similarly, in painting, her landscapes assembled as "strange a
Concourse [as] ne're was seen before,/But when the peopl'd
Ark the whole Creation bore" (stanza vi); and her portrait
of the king was "not content t' express his Outward Part,"
but "call'd out the Image of his Heart" (stanza vii). The public
value of such art, implicit in the traditional elegiac lament for
the times, is converted here into criticism of the current profana-
tion of the "Heav'nly Gift of Poesy":

> O wretched We! why were we hurry'd down
> This lubrique and adult'rate age,
> (Nay added fat Pollutions of our own)

> T' increase the steaming Ordures of the Stage?
> What can we say t' excuse our *Second Fall?*
> Let this thy *Vestal,* Heav'n, attone for all! (11. 62-67)

Dryden was no doubt aware of his own guilt in this indictment of the poetry of his time. But he might also have felt vindicated, if not by Mistress Killigrew's example, then by his Pindaric offering to her; for his adaptation of the purposes of the elegy to those of the ode is itself an illustration of that Classical ideal of art which the poem celebrates.

In its aim of imposing order upon disorder and of showing that order in man and in society is one with an all-encompassing universal order, all Dryden's poetry—the satirist's attack upon rebellion as well as the elegist's consolation of the emotionally distraught—is an ilustration of the Classical ideal of art. The heroic poem and the satire achieve this end directly by dramatizing conflict and by censuring evil; the ode, in its more self-conscious use of the phonic and structural materials of poetry, has an additional means to this end. Those odes written to be accompanied by music—"On the Death of Mr. Henry Purcell" (1696), and the two Cecilian poems (1687, 1697)— make this especially clear. In all three, music (harmony or order), as the law which governs the universe, nature, and man, is the key to both theme and technique. The ode to Purcell, for example, evolves from the fanciful notion that the composer *must* reside in heaven, for unlike his prototype, Orpheus, he would have been rejected by the chaos of Hell which could not have withstood the ordering power of his harmony to tune this "jarring Sphere." Such had also been his effect while on Earth, where he commanded the respectful silence of the "rival Crew" of composers and inspired their concord in one song of praise to himself. This conception of music as the harmonizing of contraries (*concordia discor*s) is structurally and musically announced in the opening stanza:

> Mark how the Lark and Linnet Sing,
> > With rival Notes
> They strain their warbling Throats,
> > To welcome in the Spring.
> > But in the close of Night,
> When *Philomel* begins her Heav'nly lay,
> > They cease their mutual spight,

Drink in her Musick with delight,
And list'ning and silent, and silent and list'ning, and
list'ning and silent obey.

The reader is directed to *listen* to the stanza as a representation
of Nature's harmony, whereby the "rival Notes" of the two
birds—suggested by contrasting vowels (m*a*rk, l*a*rk: l*i*nnet, s*i*ng)
—are blended in concert or "mutual spight," an effect which
is also articulated in the final line by the balanced inversion of
l and *s*, vowel and diphthong (*lis . . . sil . . . sil . . . lis*). This
cumulative sense of order according to law is emphasized in
the final rhyme "obey," which has itself the effect of reconciling
the unexpected extension and the anticipated closure of the
last line.[7]

Dryden's Cecilian odes—written for the Music Society's annual
celebration of the feast of St. Cecilia, the patroness of music—
are liable to that criticism of virtuosity of which the vulgariza-
tions of Poe and Vachel Lindsay have made the modern reader
peculiarly susceptible. But verbal orchestration on the scale of
A Song for St. Cecilia's Day and *Alexander's Feast* was an
exciting innovation in Dryden's day, and the great popularity
of the poems since then can only be attributed to their genuine
vitality. Both poems attempt to demonstrate the effects of music
upon the emotional harmony of man through phonic and rhythm-
ical approximations of the sound of instruments (trumpet, flute,
lute, violin, and the organ which St. Cecilia is supposed to
have invented). In *Alexander's Feast*, we see their ethical effects
upon man (the inspiration of divinity, bacchanalian joy, martial
zeal, pity, love, and revenge). The conception of an *ethos* in
music is combined in *Alexander's Feast* with the conception of
music as the harmonizing of human passion (*musica humana*)
with universal order (*musica mundana*). In giving men the instrument of heavenly harmony—the organ—St. Cecilia extended
the benefits of music beyond those influences which Timotheus
was able to exert upon Alexander the Great. In the conclusion
of the "Grand Chorus," these two conceptions of music are
combined as the motives of heroic action and of religious devotion:

Let old *Timotheus* yield the Prize,
Or both divide the Crown:

> He rais'd a Mortal to the Skies;
> She drew an Angel down.

Much the same point is made by the sampling of instrumental sounds in the *Song;* here also man's harmony with the universe is described in terms of the traditional analogy between musical harmony and God's creation. God is the archetypal musician; his "tuneful Voice" composed chaos into an ordered "compass of . . . Notes" or scale of being, the range of which was repeated in the perfect order of man. This idea is given not only explicit statement in the poem, but, as Earl Wasserman has brilliantly demonstrated,[8] is musically articulated in the remarkable prosody of the first stanza:

> From Harmony, from heav'nly Harmony
>   This universal Frame began.
> When Nature underneath a heap
>   Of jarring Atomes lay,
>   And cou'd not heave her Head,
> The tuneful Voice was heard from high . . . . (ll. 1-6)

The original chaos is represented in these first six lines by the absence of rhyme (*a, b, c, d, e, f*) and a distinguishable metrical plan (the lines run in lengths of 5, 4, 4, 3, 3, and 4 feet). Only with the divine command "Arise ye more than dead" (l. 7) does a recognizable order begin to appear, and then it is one which gradually works out of the chaotic middle of the stanza and through the following six lines to a perfect identity; thus lines seven and eight match in both rhyme and line length lines five and six; lines nine and ten match lines three and four; and lines eleven and twelve are identical to lines one and two:

> Arise ye more than dead.
> Then cold, and hot, and moist, and dry,
>   In order to their stations leap,
>   And MUSICK'S Pow'r obey.
> From Harmony, from heav'nly Harmony
>   This universal Frame began . . . . (ll. 7-12)

Metrically, the emerging order in the second group of six lines is an analogy of the musical conception of the first six days of God's creation. Moreover, the perfect order of the completed universe, expressed by the repeated *a* and *b* sounds, is again expressed in the three-line coda devoted to man, a microcosm, or smaller example, of that order:

From Harmony to Harmony
Through all the compass of the Notes it ran,
The Diapason closing full in Man. (ll. 13-15)

II *Translations*

The sheer bulk of Dryden's output as a translator is remarkable: the whole of Virgil—the Pastorals, the Georgics, and the *Aeneid* (1697); the whole of Persius; a portion of Juvenal (1693); from Ovid, the first book of *The Art of Love* (1709), selections from *Metamorphoses* (including all of the first and twelfth books), and the *Amores;* from Homer, Book I of the *Iliad;* and finally the imitations of Boccaccio and Chaucer which were included in the *Fables* (1700)—all this (and more, if his prose translations are considered) in the last decade of his life! There were, to be sure, economic and political reasons for this activity; translation was both a profitable enterprise and, now that there could no longer be a political motive for his work, the chief avenue of activity available to his talent.

Translation was also, however, congenial to his talent. As a satirist, Dryden conceived of his social role in Juvenalian terms—as a physician's prescribing "harsh Remedies to an inveterate Disease" (though, unlike Juvenal's, his satiric voice was seldom truly denunciatory). Ovid, he admitted in 1693, was perhaps "more according to my Genius" and therefore "more easie" than, for example, the translation of Virgil, which may nevertheless have at least partially fulfilled Dryden's lifelong ambition to produce an epic.[9] Ten years before it became a necessity, Dryden had found time to contribute translations of three epistles to an edition "by several hands" of Ovid's *Heroides* (1680), and the first and second (*Sylvae*) collections of Tonson's Miscellanies (1684 and 1685) contained selections from Ovid, Theocritus, Lucretius, and Horace. Dryden's genius, as George Saintsbury has remarked, seems always to have preferred "to accept a departure from some previous work . . . as if, in his extraordinary care for the manner of his poetical work, he felt it an advantage to be relieved of much trouble about the matter."[10] Translation, as Dryden conceived of it, was ideally suited to such a genius.

Dryden first stated his theory of translation in the Preface contributed to Tonson's publication of the *Heroides*. Generalizing, as was his custom in criticism, from the example of three predecessors in the art—Jonson, Waller, and Cowley—he speaks of three classes of translation: "Metaphrase, or turning an Authour word by word, and Line by Line, from one Language into another"; "Paraphrase, or Translation with Latitude, where the Authour is kept in view by the Translator . . . but his words are not so strictly follow'd as his sense, and that too is admitted to be amplyfied, but not alter'd"; and finally "Imitation, where the Translator . . . assumes the liberty not only to vary from the words and sence, but to forsake them both as he sees occasion" (I, 182).

The first method, he maintains, is both pedantic and impracticable since the structural differences between languages do not permit the exact translation of words, let alone the thoughts of an original; where one adds the requirements of meter and rhyme, "either perspicuity or gracefulness will frequently be wanting" (I, 183). In avoiding these difficulties, however, the "imitation" is liable to become an entirely new work, thereby doing "the greatest wrong which can be done to the Memory and Reputation of the dead" (I, 184). Dryden's view of translation comprises a mean between these two extremes. "The sence of an Authour"—and by this is meant not merely the thought of a poem, but the manner or "Spirit" of the poet, the "particular turn of Thoughts, and of Expression" which distinguishes him from others—"the sence of an Authour, generally speaking, is to be Sacred and inviolable" (I, 185). The translator is to make his own genius "conform" to that of his author, to give his thought "the same turn if our tongue will bear it, or if not, to vary but the dress"—the words and meter of the original (I, 185). To be a thorough translator, then, is to be a thorough poet.[11]

The restatement of this theory in the Preface to *Sylvae* and in the Dedication of *Examen Poeticum* considers in greater detail the individualizing features of the authors Dryden translated and thus provides a means of judging his actual practice. The hallmark of Ovid's style, for instance, is "sweetness" and luxuriance of fancy and expressions: "He avoids . . . all Synaloepha's or cutting off one Vowel when it comes before another, in the following word. So that minding only smoothness, he wants both Variety and Majesty."[12] These characteristics are, in general, opposed to the qualities of strength and variety in Dryden's own metrical practice; yet in his translation of the *Epistles* he manages even to suppress the seventeenth-century habit of eliding "gaping" vowels, and, throughout, the smooth, unvarying "Hand-gallop" of Ovid is successfully rendered. On the other hand, Dryden's imagination was similar, in its "quickness" and "fertility," to Ovid's, a fact which, Sir Walter Scott believed, led him "to add to the offences of his original."[13] For Dryden, however, invention and fancy were necessary in drawing an image of a mind either "combating between two contrary passions, or extremely discompos'd by one," and the general similarity between the style of these translations and that of his heroic plays reinforces his earlier statement that Ovid's qualities constituted "the proper wit of Dialogue or Discourse, and, consequently, of the *Drama*. . . ."[14]

Virgil, however, who "speaks not so often to us in the person of another, like *Ovid*, but in his own," makes elocution an added responsibility of the translator: "I look'd on *Virgil*, as a succinct and grave Majestick Writer," Dryden writes in the Preface to *Sylvae;* "one who weigh'd not only every thought, but every Word and Syllable. Who was still aiming to crowd his sence into as narrow a compass as possibly he cou'd; for which reason he is so very Figurative, that he requires (I may almost say) a Grammer apart to construe him. His Verse is everywhere sounding the very thing in your Ears, whose sence it bears; Yet the Numbers are perpetually varied, to increase the delight of the Reader" (I, 392). This exact propriety of thoughts and words—from which, by the way, Dryden drew his definition of wit—makes Virgil virtually untranslatable, for his words are "always figurative." He explains in the Dedication of the *Aeneid* that his chief care was with the sound of the translation; again he strove for "sweetness," avoiding synaloepha and the consonantal deadweight of monosyllables, and employing triplet rhymes, Alexandrines, and polysyllabic Latinate diction. The latter provided not only musical "ornament," but a rich source of metaphor; for, as William Frost has remarked, Latin was a "living language" to Dryden, one whose buried metaphors lay "just beneath the surface," and thus imparted a special vitality to its derivatives in English.[15] Moreover, as the Virgilian echoes of *Absalom and Achitophel* indicate, Dryden was sympathetic to Virgil's theme, to the Roman conception of civilization as the order inherent in a people's obedience to a hero-prince. By such means, Dryden produced what he himself considered "a passable beauty" in the absence of the original, though the effect of its "Heroics" still seems synthetic to the modern reader.

The translations of Juvenal and Persius are remarkably fresh, however; if the elevated dignity required by epic lay beyond the range of English, the trenchant and commonplace diction proper to satire did not. Avoiding the inherent difficulties of satiric topicality, he took greater liberties with the originals, producing "somewhat . . . betwixt a Paraphrase and Imitation," and endeavoring to make the author speak "that kind of *English*, which he wou'd have spoken had he liv'd in *England*, and had Written to this age."[16] The effect is perhaps most vividly demonstrated by that passage of the sixth satire against women, a passage which describes in mock-heroic terms Empress Messalina's lustful indulgence in "the Pleasures of the Night." Rising from the emperor's bed, she "Strode from the Palace, with an eager pace,/To cope with a more Masculine Embrace:/Muffl'd she march'd, like *Juno* in a Clowd . . . To the known Brothel-house":

> Prepar'd for fight, expectingly she lies,
> With heaving Breasts, and with desiring Eyes:
> Still as one drops, another takes his place
> And baffled still succeeds to like disgrace. (11. 163-89)

As Dryden explained in his prose argument of the poem, "my Author makes their Lust the most Heroick of their Vices"; accordingly, he ironically renders it as the "Fire" which impels the hero to martial prowess.

The freedom and the apparent ease with which Juvenal and Persius were adapted to the language and temper of the seventeenth century were no doubt severely curtailed in the arduous three years spent in the attempt to make the Virgilian epic acceptable to an age of rationalism. It was probably with a sense of relief then that Dryden returned to the more personal mode of "paraphrase" and "imitation" in his last and most generally admired collection of translations, *The Fables*. His Preface to this volume suggests that he was guided even in the selection of materials by his natural inclination, and, though interrupted by illness, that the work was a source of joy to him. The long-suppressed desire simply to *tell a story* was at last realized here, and the work which was intended to be "but a Lodge" grew to the proportions of a house. He began by rendering the first book of the *Iliad* which, in its Restoration picture of the domestic habits of the Olympian Gods, may suggest something of the mock-heroic treatment, but it also conveys that sense of Homeric "Vigour" which Dryden speaks of in his Preface. He turned next to the related materials in the twelfth book of Ovid's *Metamorphoses;* then to the argument between Ulysses and Ajax in the thirteenth book; the digression on Pythagorean philosophy in the fifteenth ("the Master-piece of the whole *Metamorphoses*," Dryden considered it); and to five other stories from the earlier books, including "Pygmalion and the Statue" and "Baucus and Philemon," the warmly human picture of decent poverty which Swift later travestied. Ovid suggested Chaucer (represented by retellings of four of the *Canterbury Tales* and the pseudo-Chaucerian "The Flower and the Leaf"), and Chaucer, in turn, his contemporary Boccaccio (represented by three tales of the *Decameron*). In addition to the superb Preface, the volume also included "Alexander's Feast," and the graceful tribute "To my Honour'd Kinsman, John Driden, of Chesterton." But of all the verse the translations of Chaucer are of the greatest interest.

Although the twentieth century has little difficulty justifying its preference for reading Chaucer in the original, Dryden's reasons for modernizing him are not only understandable but a tribute to his critical judgment. The seventeenth-century veneration of Chaucer appears to have been pedantic and antiquarian rather than literary, or at best a type of literary snobbery which Dryden describes in his Preface as a miserly hoarding of "their Grandam Gold, only to look on it themselves, and hinder others from making use of it" (IV, 1459). Probably more widespread, however, was the view of Chaucer as a "dry, old-fashion'd Wit, not worth receiving" (IV, 1457). He was, moreover, read in a corrupt text and without the linguistic knowledge by which his numbers become something more than "the rude sweetness of a *Scotch* Tune." Dryden, too, suffered from the prejudices of his age; Chaucer, he believed, wrote in "the Infancy of our Poetry" (and "no thing is brought to Perfection at the first"), before the language was adequate to express his thoughts and before "Equality of Numbers" was either known or practiced (IV, 1453). But he is "the Father of *English* Poetry"—standing in the same relation to us as Homer and Virgil to the Greeks and Romans—"a perpetual Fountain of good Sense," and "a Man of a most wonderful comprehensive Nature," encompassing the manners and humors of the entire English nation (IV, 1452, 1455). Dryden aimed to make these virtues more widely known to those of his countrymen "who understand Sense and Poetry, as well as they [the scholars] when that Poetry and Sense is put into Words which they understand" (IV, 1459), and he justified his view in terms of a utilitatian conception of language: "When an ancient Word for its Sound and Significancy deserves to be reviv'd, I have that reasonable Veneration for Antiquity, to restore it. All beyond this is Superstition. Words are not like Landmarks, so sacred as never to be remov'd: Customs are chang'd, and even Statutes are silently repeal'd, when the Reason ceases for which they were enacted" (IV, 1458).

Two illustrations from the translation of the "Wife of Bath's Tale" may serve to indicate the nature and scope of Dryden's changes. The first describes the violent act which serves as motivation of the tale:

CHAUCER	DRYDEN'S TRANSLATION
And so bifel it that the kyng Arthour	It so befel in this King *Arthur's* Reign,
Hadde in his hous a lusty bachelor	A lusty Knight was pricking o'er the Plain;
	A Batchelor he was, and of the courtly Train.
That on a day cam ridynge fro ryver;	It happen'd as he rode, a Damsel gay
And happed that, allone as she was born,	In Russet-Robes to Market took her way;
He saugh a mayde walkynge hym biforn,	Soon on the Girl he cast an amorous Eye,
	So strait she walk'd, and on her Pasterns high
	If seeing her behind he lik'd her Pace,
Of which mayde anon, maugree hir heed,	Now turning short he better lik'd her Face:

By verray force, he rafte hire
  maydenhed.[17]

He lights in hast, and full of
  Youthful Fire,
By Force accomplish'd his ob-
  scene Desire. (11. 46-56)

What for Chaucer was simply a necessary part of the plot, to be compressed in as few lines as possible, becomes in Dryden a stock scene—consciously "literary," as the Spenserian echoes of the second and tenth lines and the quaint phrase "Pasterns high" indicate—the two figures of which are formally "set" in the introductory triplet and couplet. Completely absent, except for the explicit judgment of Dryden's last line, is the sense of cruelty in the knight's casualness (in the original, he comes up-on his prey "allone as she was born," as he returns from hawk-ing, "fro ryver"). Instead, Dryden exploits the humorous poten-tial of the scene, expanding Chaucer's view of the maide "walk-ynge hym biforn" (and possibly misreading his "maugree hir heed" as a reference to her "Face") into five lines of lascivious leering and the first line of the final couplet.

This change is not adequately appreciated, however, until it is seen in relation to the following passage, in which the knight is later brought to bed with the loathly hag:

CHAUCER	DRYDEN'S TRANSLATION
Greet was the wo the knyght hadde in his thoght, Whan he was with his wyf abedde ybroght; He walweth and he turneth to and fro.	To Bed they went, the Bride-groom and the Bride: Was never such an ill-pair'd Couple ty'd. Restless he toss'd and tumbled to and fro, And rowl'd, and wriggled further off; for Woe.
His olde wyf lay smylynge ever-mo, And seyde, "O deere housbonde, Fareth every knyght thus with his wyf as ye?	The good old Wife lay smiling by his Side, And caught him in her quiv'ring Arms, and cry'd, When you my ravish'd Prede-cessor saw, You were not then become this Man of Straw;

Had you been such, you might
have scap'd the Law. }

Is this the lawe of kyng Arthures hous?	Is this the Custom of King Arthur's Court?
Is every knight of his so dangerous?	Are all Round-Table Knights of such a sort?
I am youre owene love and eek youre wyf;	Remember I am she who sav'd your Life,
I am she which that saved hath youre lyf.[18]	Your loving, lawful, and complying Wife (11. 344-54).

Here Dryden has adopted—at least approximately—Chaucer's third, fourth, seventh, eighth, and ninth lines. The sense of the vivid but obscure "walweth" requires an additional line in Dryden's version, as does Chaucer's fourth line, in the rendering of which the word "good" apparently compensated for Dryden's failure to pronounce the final *e* of "olde"; Chaucer's sixth and eighth lines are combined, with some loss of the irony of the original, in Dryden's eleventh. Here again, however, the translation is more deliberately comic, and it is organized in terms of the paradox announced in the first couplet: "To Bed they went, the Bridegroom and the Bride" (common purpose): "an ill-pair'd Couple" (the knight's abhorrence of his bride). Dryden's hag is much more genuinely puzzled by her husband's behavior than Chaucer's, for the contrast between what she interprets as his embarrassment and the real reason for his restlessness ("Woe") is ironically emphasized in the fourth line, and then further developed in the triplet. Clearly her reference to her "ravish'd Predecessor" increases the ironic effect of the passage, recalling from Dryden's earlier expansion the knight's "hast" and "Youthful Fire."

Not all Dryden's liberties with Chaucer have weathered the changes in seventeenth-century taste as well as the two examples just cited. For better or worse, however, every translation embodies the peculiar limitations of the age for which it is written—and this is especially true of Dryden's Chaucerian "imitations." The chivalric love of Chaucer's Knight's Tale" becomes "heroical" in Dryden's "Palamon and Arcite"; the fox in the "Nun's Priest's Tale" takes on clearly recognizable Puritan features in

"The Cock and the Fox"; and the "Prologue" portrait of a Wicliffite "persoun" becomes a "Character" of the seventeenth-century nonjuring Anglican who refused to abandon his allegiance
to the Stuart James II.

It is clear, however, that Dryden believed he was doing with
Chaucer's tales what Chaucer had done before him with his
sources. His discovery that the "Knight's Tale" was "written before the time of *Boccace*" does not preclude its being "an Original" that "has receiv'd many Beauties by passing through his
[Chaucer's] Noble Hands" (IV. 1461). Dryden believed he had
"a Soul congenial" to Chaucer's, that they were "conversant in
the same Studies" (Philosophy, "philology," and astrology), and
he was able to sympathize with Chaucer's satire of the vices of
the clergy. Indeed, if Austin Dobbins is correct, Chaucer's own
Wicliffite opposition to ecclesiastical interference in politics is
precisely parallel to Dryden's criticism of the Anglican juror.[19]

It is in this very confrontation of the present and the past,
and in his reaffirmation of the past as order or value, that the
real significance of *The Fables* and of the greatest part of Dryden's translation consists. And Dryden's reaffirmation matters,
as Reuben Brower has said, "because it is a poet's affirmation,
realized in the shaping of new modes of expression and in the
writing of poetry which is imaginatively various and unified."[20]

Conclusion

There is little question of the security of Dryden's place in English literary history. "To him we owe the improvement, perhaps the completion of our metre, the refinement of our language, and much of the correctness of our sentiments,"[1] declared Samuel Johnson, the spokesman of the literary generation which Dryden inaugurated. Much the same claim for him is made in our own time by T. S. Eliot: "We cannot fully enjoy or rightly estimate a hundred years of English poetry unless we fully enjoy Dryden."[2] It is hoped that the preceding chapters at least partially attest to the significance of the literary virtues mentioned by Dr. Johnson; nevertheless, it may seem rather faint praise to celebrate Dryden in the name of an age which is synonymous with artistic restraint and intellectual commitment and acceptance. Dryden was committed to the assumptions of Neoclassicism —to monarchy, to the couplet, to the lofty ideals of the heroic and the sublime; what distinguishes him from all but the greatest of his literary descendants was his ability to function freely within those assumptions. "Luckily for himself, his age, and the history of English poetry," writes Bernard Schilling, "he was free though committed, at ease in conformity—able therefore, to do as he pleased."[3]

As an apology for exhuming the works of Chaucer, Dryden wrote in the Preface to *The Fables* that "Mankind is ever the same, and nothing lost out of Nature, though every thing is alter'd" (IV. 1455). This recognition of temporal change operating within the *sameness* of Nature—within order—was the authority for Dryden's Neoclassical freedom, not only in his translations, but everywhere in his writing. It authorized the creation, through his own metrical and linguistic practices, of standards of correctness by which, nevertheless, a John Donne was assimilable into the Augustan literary hierarchy. It permitted both his respectful attention to the Neoclassical "rules" (he hoped only "that poetry may not go backward") and the bold departures from them in an *All for Love*; it sanctioned the noble eloquence and the heroic reverberations peculiar to his satire; and it fostered that flexibility of mind which—now that it is rightly seen as the alternative to rigidity—is not only the means to a sympathetic reading of him, but the motive of his great variety. With what appears to be a sense of complete fulfillment, Dryden *worked* the assumptions of his age, and in doing so extracted values which few of his successors realized except by following his example.

Notes and References

Chapter One

1. *"Brief Lives," Chiefly of Contemporaries, set down by John Aubrey, between the Years 1669 & 1696,* ed. Andrew Clark (Oxford, 1898), I, 241.

2. "A Defence of an Essay of Dramatic Poesy" (1668), *Essays of John Dryden,* ed. W. P. Ker New York, 1961), I, 116, hereafter cited as *Essays.*

3. Sir Walter Scott, *The Life of John Dryden* offers the most ample collection of such detail. This *Life,* in many ways the clearest picture of the man, has recently been edited and corrected by Bernard Kreissman for Bison Books (Lincoln, Nebraska, 1963). James Osborn, *John Dryden: Some Biographical Facts and Problems,* New York, 1940) reviews the early biographies of the poet.

4. The date is speculative, based on the date of baptism, August 14, recorded in the parish register. See Charles E. Ward's note on the poet's birth in *The Life of John Dryden*—hereafter cited as *Life*—(Chapel Hill, N. C., 1961), p. 333, my source of most facts concerning Dryden's life.

5. See Scott's *Life,* p. 21, n. 2.

6. Inscription of Dryden's translation of Persius' Fifth Satire (1693), *The Poems of John Dryden,* ed. James Kinsley (Oxford, 1958), II, 771. Hereafter cited as *Poems.*

7. See the "Commentary" on the poem in *The Works of John Dryden,* ed. Edward Niles Hooker and H. T. Swedenberg, Jr. (Berkeley, Calif., 1956), I, 182. Hereafter cited as *Works.*

8. *Life,* "Appendix B."

9. *Works,* I, 20, The evidence of Dryden's having worked for Herringman is thoroughly reviewed but found inconclusive by James Osborn in *John Dryden: Some Biographical Facts,* pp. 168-83.

10. "The Vindication of the Duke of Guise" (1683), included

in *Dryden: The Dramatic Works*, ed. Montague Summers (London, 1932), V, 299.

11. *Life*, p. 31.

12. *Ibid.*, p. 339. Sprat's *History of the Royal Society* (1667) is quoted in Richard Foster Jones, "Science and English Prose Style in the Third Quarter of the Seventeenth Century," *The Seventeenth Century* (Stanford, Calif., 1951), p. 85; see also pp. 99-100.

13. *Essays*, I, 124.

14. Allardyce Nicoll, *A History of Restoration Drama: 1660-1700*, 2nd ed. (Cambridge, 1928), "Appendix A." Nicoll's "Handlist of Restoration Plays" ("Appendix C") is my authority for the production dates of Dryden's plays.

15. In the "Connection of *The Indian Emperor* to *The Indian Queen*," Dryden claims to have written "part" of the play. See *Dramatic Works*, I, 273. See also John Harrington Smith, "The Dryden- Howard Collaboration," *Studies in Philology*, LI (1954), 55-74; and *Works*, VIII, 283.

16. See Samuel Pordage's "Azaria and Hushai" in *Anti Achitophel: Three Verse Replies to Absalom and Achitophel by John Dryden*, ed. Harold Whitmore Jones, Scholars' Facsimilies and Reprints (Gainesville, Florida, 1961), p. 103.

17. *Life*, pp. 76-77.

18. Charles was born August 27, 1666, Erasmus on May 2, 1669; John's birth is conjectured to have been in 1668. See *Life*, pp. 341, n. 4; 67; 344-45, n. 2.

19. *Ibid.*, p. 45.

20. See James Osborn, *John Dryden: Some Biographical Facts and Problems,* pp. 184-91.

21. *Life*, p. 69.

22. See *Life*, p. 83; Scott, *Life*, p. 121. Sam Briscoe's "Key" is conveniently available in a Barron's Educational Series volume, *The Rehearsal: The Critic* (Great Neck, N. Y., 1960).

23. George Saintsbury, *Dryden* (New York, n.d.), p. 52.

24. *Life*, p. 104.

25. *Ibid.*, p. 108.

26. *Dramatic Works*, IV, 84.

27. *Life*, p. 118.

28. *Essays*, II, 38.

29. The complaint is discussed by James Osborn, *John Dryden*:

Notes and References

Some Biographical Facts, pp. 184-91.

30. Though not cited in the complaint of the managers of the King's Company, Dryden's *The Kind Keeper* had been produced by the Duke's Company in 1678.

31. Hugh Macdonald, *John Dryden: A Bibliography of Early Editions and of Drydeniana* (New York, 1950), p. 26.

32. *Poems,* I, 310.

33. Charles E. Ward, ed., *The Letters of John Dryden, with Letters Addressed to Him* (Durham, N. C., 1942), pp. 20-22.

34. *Life,* p. 211.

35. *Ibid.,* p. 197.

36. *Dramatic Works,* VI, 30.

37. *Poems,* III, 1424.

38. *Life,* p. 370, n. 8.

Chapter Two

1. *Poems,* I, 16, 11. 21-28. Unless otherwise indicated, subsequent citations of Dryden's poems are from this edition and are referred to parenthetically either by line number or by volume and page.

2. "On the Death of Mrs. Killigrew: The Perfecting of a Genre," *Studies in Philology,* XLIV (1947), 521-22. For the similarities in thought and manner between Dryden's poem and others in *Lachrymae Musarum,* see the "Commentary" on the poem in *Works,* I, 172, 174 ff.

3. *Essays,* I, 31, 52.

4. *Spectator,* No. 160 (September 3, 1711), Everyman Library (London, 1911), I, 283.

5. "The Tendency toward Platonism in Neo-Classical Esthetics," *English Literary History,* I, (1934), 101. For the effect of this aesthetic on the conservative tradition of prosody see Paul Fussell, Jr., *Theory of Prosody in Eighteenth Century England,* Connecticut College Monograph, No. 5 (New London, Conn., 1954), p. 52.

6. W. K. Wimsatt and Cleanth Brooks, *Literary Criticism: A Short History* (New York, 1957), p. 222.

7. P. A. Duhamel, "The Logic and Rhetoric of Peter Ramus," *Modern Philology,* XLVI (1949), 163.

8. *The Seventeenth Century Background* (London, 1942), pp. 87-88.

9. Quoted by Wimsatt and Brooks, p. 228.

10. *Studies in Seventeenth-Century Poetic* (Madison, Wisc., 1950), p. 131.

11. See George Williamson, "The Restoration Revolt against Enthusiasm," *Studies in Philology,* XXX (1933), 571-603.

12. Quoted in *Works,* I, 190-91.

13. Preface to *Annus Mirabilis, Essays,* I, 11.

14. See *Works,* I, 189, n. 7.

15. Edward, Earl of Clarendon, *The History of the Rebellion and Civil Wars in England* (Oxford, 1840), II, 900.

16. *The Eclogues and Georgics of Virgil,* trans. T. F. Royds, Everyman's Library (London, 1950), p. 24. For Dryden's translation of the passage, see *Poems,* II, 887, ll. 5-12.

17. H. T. Swedenberg, Jr., "Englands Joy: *Astraea Redux* in its Setting," *Studies in Philology,* L (1953), 34.

18. See Rosemond Tuve, "The Hymn on the Morning of Christ's Nativity," *Images & Themes in Five Poems by Milton* (Cambridge, 1957), pp. 37-72; and Samuel Chew, *The Virtues Reconciled* (Toronto, 1947), p. 59.

19. Earl Wasserman, "Dryden: Epistle to Charleton," *The Subtler Language* (Baltimore, 1959), p. 16. I have drawn heavily from Professor Wasserman's explication in the remainder of this paragraph.

20. *Ibid.,* pp. 21, 30.

21. *Ibid.,* p. 33.

22. See the "Commentary" on the poem in *Works,* I, 258.

23. *Ibid.,* p. 259. See also Edward Niles Hooker, "The Purpose of Dryden's *Annus Mirabilis," Huntington Library Quarterly,* X (1946), 49-67.

24. See the textual note to ll. 417-20 in *Poems.*

Chapter Three

1. *Essays,* I, 27. Unless otherwise indicated, subsequent citations of Dryden's essays are from this edition, and are referred to parenthetically by volume and page number.

2. See George Williamson, "The Occasion of 'An Essay of

Dramatic Poesy,'" *Modern Philology*, XLIV (1946), 1-9.

3. Wimsatt and Brooks, p. 184. See Charles Kaplan, *The Explicator*, XIII (March, 1950), No. 36.

4. Frank L. Huntley, *On Dryden's "Essay of Dramatic Poesy,"* *University of Michigan Contributions in Modern Philology*, No. 16 (Ann Arbor, Mich., 1951), p. 12.

5. Since Malone, the four speakers in the *Essay* have, with general agreement, been identified as follows: Crites with Dryden's brother-in-law, Sir Robert Howard; Eugenius with his patron Lord Buckhurst; Lisideius with Sir Charles Sedley; and Neander with Dryden himself. For a cogent argument against the second identification, see George R. Noyes, "Crites in Dryden's *Essay of Dramatic Poesy*," *Modern Language Notes*, XXXVIII (1923), 333-37; for a sceptical view of the identification of any of the four speakers, see Huntley, *op. cit.*, and his earlier article, "On the Persons in Dryden's *Essay of Dramatic Poesy*," *Modern Language Notes*, LXIII (1948), 88-95.

6 *Poetics*, IX, Bywater translation.

7. Walter Jackson Bate, *Criticism: The Major Texts* (New York, 1952), p. 4. The "Introduction" to the first section of this volume offers an unusually lucid discussion of the Classical–NeoClassical tradition.

8. *Essays*, "Introduction," I, xxii-xxiii.

9. See Richard Foster Jones, "Science and Criticism in the Neo-Classical Age of English Literature," *The Seventeenth Century*, pp. 45-46.

10. Printed in *Dryden and Howard: 1664-1668*, ed. D. D. Arundell (Cambridge, 1929), p. 94.

11. Dryden summarized the course of the dispute at the end of his "Defence," in its formal conclusion. See *Essays*, I, 133. D. D. Arundell, *op. cit.*, reprints the pertinent texts of both disputants.

12. These words, applied to this context by Hoyt Trowbridge, are from Dryden's *Life of Plutarch*. See Trowbridge's "The Place of Rules in Dryden's Criticism," *Modern Philology*, XLIV (1946), 92, an article I am much indebted to in this paragraph.

13. *Ibid.*, p. 94.

14. Wimsatt and Brooks, p. 229.

15. See George Williamson, *The Proper Wit of Poetry* (Chicago, 1961), p. 87.

16. *Essays,* "Introduction," I, xvi.
17. *The Seventeenth Century Background,* p. 220.
18. *Dryden,* p. 123.

Chapter Four

1. See Allardyce Nicoll, *A History of Restoration Drama,* "Appendix A."
2. See Nicoll's "Hand-list of Restoration Plays," *Ibid.,* "Appendix C."
3. "A Parallel of Poetry and Painting" (1695), *Essays,* II, 152.
4. *Dramatic Essays of the Neoclassic Age,* ed. Henry Hitch Adams and Baxter Hathaway (New York, 1950), p. 190.
5. *Restoration Comedy* (Oxford, 1938), p. 23.
6. "Restoration Comedy: The Reality and the Myth," *Explorations* (New York, 1947), pp. 161-64.
7. *Dramatic Works,* ed. Montague Summers. Since this edition does not provide line numbers, references to the plays will be cited by act and page number in parentheses, those to Dryden's prefaces and dedications by volume and page number.
8. Knights, p. 163; Dobrée, p. 106.
9. "To the Reader," prefacing *"The Faithful Shepherdess,* in *Beaumont and Fletcher,* ed. J. St. Loe Strachey (London, n.d.), II, 321.
10. *Essays,* I, 72. For Dryden's opinion of his own abilities as a comic writer, see Preface to *An Evening's Love* (1671), *ibid.,* I, 135; "A Defence of an Essay of Dramatic Poesy" (1668), *ibid.,* I, 116; and the Dedication to *Aureng-Zebe* (1676), Dramatic *Works,* IV, 84.
11. *Essays,* I, 69.
12. This does not exhaust the list of Dryden's comic couples. Florimel and Celadon, in *Secret Love* (1667), perhaps his most attractive couple, confine their tricks, however, to two sisters, Olinda and Sabina; and Wildblood and Jacintha, and Bellamy and Theodosia in *An Evening's Love* (1668), are accomplices, not antagonists, as are also Aurelian and Laura, and Camillo and Violetta, in *The Assignation* (1672).
13. *Essays,* I, 138-40.
14. *Ibid.,* I, 85.
15. See Kathleen M. Lynch, *The Social Mode of Restoration*

Comedy, University of Michigan Publications in Language and Literature, III (New York, 1926), pp. 17, 19.

16. *Essays*, I, 84.
17. Preface to *An Evening's Love, Essays*, I, 139.
18. "Defence of the Epilogue," *Essays*, I, 176.
19. "Restoration Comedy: The Reality and the Myth," pp. 154-55, 163, n. 1.
20. Dryden's sources dictated the locale of the plays. For a discussion of the sources, see Summers' introduction to each of the plays in the *Dramatic Works*, and Ned B. Allen, *The Sources of John Dryden's Comedies, University of Michigan Publications in Language and Literature*, XVI (Ann Arbor, Mich., 1935).
21. Scott C. Osborn, "Heroical Love in Dryden's Heroic Drama," *Publications of the Modern Language Association*, LXXIII (1958), 481. From the voluminous literature on this subject, see, for the French source of this Platonism, B. J. Pendlebury, *Dryden's Heroic Plays: A Study of the Origins* (London, 1923), and Summers' introduction to the first volume of *Dramatic works;* for English sources, see Nicoll, *A History of Restoration Drama*, Chap. II, and Kathleen M. Lynch, "Conventions of Platonic Drama in the Heroic Plays of Orrey and Dryden," *Publications of the Modern Language Association*, XLIV (1929), 461-70.
22. See Mildred E. Hartsock, "Dryden's Plays: A Study in Ideas," *Seventeenth Century Studies*, 2nd. Ser., ed. Robert Shafer (Princeton, N. J., 1937), p. 89.
23. Scott C. Osborn, pp. 481, 489.
24. *Ibid.*, p. 489.
25. "Of Heroic Plays," *Essays*, I, 157. See also the Dedication to *The Conquest of Granada, Dramatic Works*, III, 17-18.
26. Hoxie Neal Fairchild, *The Noble Savage* (New York, 1928), p. 29.
27. *The Herculean Hero in Marlowe, Chapman, Shakespeare and Dryden* (London, 1962), p. 167.
28. *Paideia: The Idea of Greek Culture* (New York, 1943), II, 53.
29. *Ibid.*, p. 56.
30. *Waith*, pp. 184-85.
31. See Arthur C. Kirsch, "The Significance of Dryden's *Aureng-Zebe*," *English Literary History*, XXIX (1962), 160-74.

32. *Essays*, I, 100-101.

33. Kirsch, pp. 174, 166.

34. The phrase is Stanley Edgar Hyman's in *Poetry and Criticism* (New York, 1961), p. 50.

35. Preface to *Troilus and Cressida, Essays*, I, 210.

36. "Tragic Theory in the Late 17th Century," *English Literary History*, XXIX (1962), 306-23. Dryden dealt specifically with Rapin's affective theory in the Preface to *Troilus and Cressida* (1679). The older Aristotelian fabulist theory, as expressed by Thomas Rymer, prompted Dryden's "Heads of an Answer to Rymer," published posthumously in 1711.

37. See Bruce King, "Dryden's Intent in *All for Love*," *College English*, XXIV (1963), 270.

38. *Waith*, p. 195.

39. *Ibid.*, p. 200.

Chapter Five

1. *Lives of the English Poets* (Everyman Library), I, 198. See the dedication of *Aureng-Zebe, The Dramatic Works*, IV, 84; also "A Discourse concerning the Original and Progress of Satire" (1693), *Essays*, II, 38.

2. *Dramatic Works*, III, 416.

3. "The Preface," in *Poems*, I, 311. Subsequent references to Dryden's poems are from this source, and will be cited parenthetically by page or line number.

4. Austin Warren, *Rage for Order* (Chicago, 1948), p. 40. The view of Augustan satire and burlesque as an escape from "the stylistic restrictions of Great Poetry" was first coherently stated by Professor Warren.

5. "A Discourse concerning . . . Satire," *Essays*, II, 93.

6. *Ibid.*, II, 94, 93, 101.

7. *The Poetry of John Dryden* (New York, 1920), p. 185.

8. Warren, p. 40.

9. "The Augustan Mode in English Poetry," *English Literary History*, XX (1953), 2.

10. Van Doren, p. 165.

11. *Ibid.*, I, 205. See also Dryden's epilogue to Thomas Southerne's *The Loyal Brother* (1682), *ibid.*, I, 248: "Tho Nonsense

is a nauseous heavy Mass,/The Vehicle call'd Faction makes it pass."

12. See the summary of evidence concerning the authorship of *Mac Flecknoe* in the "Appendix" of Van Doren's *John Dryden*. On the course of Shadwell's quarrel with Dryden, see Daniel M. McKeithan, "The Occasion of *Mac Flecknoe*," *Publications of the Modern Language Association*, XLVII (1932), 766-71.

13. McKeithan, p. 770.

14. "A Discourse concerning . . . Satire," *Essays*, I, 79.

15. "The Muse of Satire," *The Yale Review*, XLI (1951), 80-92.

16. W. D. Christie's note to the line in *The Poetical Works of John Dryden* (London, 1907), p. 146.

17. See J. E. Tanner, "The Messianic Image in *Mac Flecknoe*," *Modern Language Notes*, LXXVI (1961), 220-23. The Elijah-Elisha allusion was first recognized by Baird W. Whitlock, "Elijah-Elisha in Dryden's 'Mac Flecknoe,'" *Modern Language Notes*, LXX (1955), 19-20.

18. "To the Reader," prefacing *Absalom and Achitophel*, *Poems*, I, 215.

19. *Essays*, II, 92-93; *Poems*, I, 248, 1. 463.

20. "Mock-Heroic: *Mac Flecknoe*," *Seventeenth Century English Poetry*, ed. William R. Keast (New York, 1962), p. 433.

21. "To the Reader," prefacing *Absalom and Achitophel*, *Poems*, I, 216.

22. See Morris Freedman, "Dryden's Miniature Epic," *Journal of English and German Philology*, LVII (1958), 211-19; Albert Ball, "Charles II: Dryden's Christian Hero," *Modern Philology*, LIX (1961), 32.

23. *Essays*, II, 108.

24. Richard F. Jones, "The Originality of *Absalom and Achitophel*," *Modern Language Notes*, XLVI (1931), 211-18.

25. "Dedication of the *Aeneis*," *Essays*, II, 171.

26. The physiological background pertinent to *Absalom and Achitophel* has been thoroughly surveyed by Ruth Wallerstein in "To Madness Near Allied: Shaftesbury and His Place in the Design and Thought of *Absalom and Achitophel*," *Huntington Library Quarterly*, VI (1943), 445-71.

27. See Morris Freedman, "Dryden's Miniature Epic," pp. 211-19.

28. See A. B. Chambers, "Absalom and Achitophel: Christ and

Satan," *Modern Language Notes,* LXXIV (1959), 592-96.

29. *Dryden and the Conservative Myth: A Reading of Absalom and Achitophel,* (New Haven, Conn., 1961), p. 283.

30. *Ibid.,* p. 138.

31. "Discourse concerning . . . Satire," *Essays,* II, 80.

Chapter Six

1. Richard Hooker, *Of the Laws of Ecclesiastical Polity,* Everyman's Library, "Preface," iii, 2 (London, 1954), I, 95.

2. Louis Bredvold, *The Intellectual Milieu of John Dryden, University of Michigan Publications in Language and Literature,* XII, (Ann Arbor, 1934), p. 17-35.

3. Louis Bredvold, *The Best of Dryden* (New York, 1933), pp. xxxi-xxxii.

4. *The Intellectual Milieu,* pp. 76-85.

5. Quoted by Kinsley in the notes to *Religio Laici* in *Poems,* IV, 1932. Subsequent references to the poems in this chapter are from this source, and are cited parenthetically by line number.

6. The Preface to *Religio Laici, ibid.,* I, 310.

7. Bredvold, *The Intellectual Milieu,* p. 121.

8. *Ibid.,* p. 126.

9. Edward Niles Hooker, "Dryden and the Atoms of Epicurus," *English Literary History,* XXIV (1957), 177-90.

10. Thomas H. Fujimura, "Dryden's *Religio Laici:* An Anglican Poem," *Publications of the Modern Language Association,* LXXVI (1961), 207.

11. Elias J. Chiasson, "Dryden's Apparent Scepticism in *Religio Laici,*" *Harvard Theological Review,* LIV (1961), 212.

12. Fujimura, p. 209.

13. Fujimura, pp. 211-12; Chiasson, p. 216.

14. Fujimura, p. 207.

15. It is not entirely clear whether "startle" and "stagger" are to be understood as contrasting or as generally equivalent terms. In either case, however, the ultimate meaning is the same: i.e., reason is *aroused* to activity; or reason, after a moment of confusion, resumes its activity. For the meaning of "startle" as "arouse," "excite," see the *Oxford English Dictionary,* "startle," def. 7.

16. Chiasson, p. 218.
17. Professor Bredvold in *The Intellectual Milieu of John Dryden*, p. 103, suggests that Dryden alludes in these lines to the "gossip current that Simon was intentionally undermining the whole Christian religion," an insinuation which he rejects as "without foundation." Bredvold's remark, however, is based on a quotation of the passage which omits the initial conjunction "For," and thus fails to recognize the passage as an explanation of Dryden's reference of Simon as a "Matchless" author (1. 228) in the preceding paragraph. Such praise would hardly be forthcoming to an atheist, but it is quite proper for an alleged critic of Catholic infallibility.

Chapter Seven

1. *Poems*, IV, 1446. Subsequent references to Dryden's poems are to this edition and are parenthetically cited by volume and page or by line numbers.
2. *The Poetry of John Dryden*, pp. 237-38.
3. "Life of Dryden," *Lives of the Poets*, Everyman's Library (London, 1954), I, 260.
4. *The Spectator*, No. 160 (September 3, 1711)
5. Preface to *Sylvae: or the Second Part of Poetical Miscellanies* (1685), *Poems*, I, 400.
6. See Ruth Wallerstein, *Studies in Seventeenth-Century Poetic*, pp. 25, 64, and her analysis of the Killigrew ode (pp. 137-41) from which I have drawn in this and the following paragraph.
7. Earl Wasserman also notes the joining of *lark-linnet* sounds in the dipthong of "rivalry," "the chiastic arrangement of the *s* and *w* sounds" in third and fourth lines, and, in the second line of the second stanza, "the consistent recession of vowels": "They Sung no more, or only Sung his Fame." See his essay "Pope's Ode for Musick," *English Literary History*, XXVIII (1961), 164-65, to which I am also indebted for the analysis of Dryden's *Song for St. Cecilia's Day*.
8. *Ibid.*, pp. 165-69.
9. See *Absalom and Achitophel*, "To the Reader," *Poems*, I, 216, and the Dedication of *Examen Poeticum* (1693), *Poems*, II, 795.
10. *Dryden*, pp. 136-37.

11. See Preface to *Sylvae, Poems,* I, 392.

12. *Ibid.,* I, 393; see also *Poems,* II, 795.

13. *The Life of John Dryden,* p. 441.

14. Preface to *Annus Mirabilis, Poems,* I, 47.

15. *Dryden and the Art of Translation* (New Haven, Conn., 1955), p. 81.

16. "Discourse concerning . . . Satire," *Poems,* II, 668-69.

17. *The Poetical Works of Chaucer,* ed. F. N. Robinson (Boston, 1933), 11. 882-88.

18. *Ibid.,* 11. 1083-92.

19. "Dryden's 'Character of a Good Parson': Background and Interpretation," *Studies in Philology,* LIII (1956), 51-59.

20. *Alexander Pope: The Poetry of Allusion* (Oxford, 1959), pp. 2-3.

Conclusion

1. *Lives of the English Poets* (Everyman Library), I, 262

2. *Selected Essays* (New York, 1950), p. 265.

3. "Introduction," *Dryden: A Collection of Critical Essays* (Englewood Cliffs, N. J., 1963), p. 4.

Selected Bibliography

BIBLIOGRAPHIES

Macdonald, Hugh. *John Dryden: A Bibliography of Early Editions and of Drydeniana.* New York: Oxford University Press, 1950. Indispensable not only for bibliographical information on Dryden's works, but also for full particulars on works by other authors relating to Dryden.

Monk, Samuel Holt. *John Dryden: A List of Critical Studies Published from 1895 to 1948.* Minneapolis: University of Minnesota Press, 1950. A listing of 768 items arranged under general categories and under separate works within those categories; indexed.

PRIMARY SOURCES

1. Editions of Complete Works

Hooker, Edward Niles, H. T. Swedenberg, Jr. *et al.,* eds. *The William Andrews Clark Edition of Dryden's Works.* Berkeley, Calif.: University of California Press, 1956—. Vol. I, *Poems:1649-1680;* Vol. VIII, *Plays: The Wild Gallant; The Rival Ladies; The Indian Queen.* A magnificent edition of Dryden's writings in prose and verse.

Scott, Sir Walter, ed. *The Works of John Dryden.* Edinburgh, 1808. 18 vols. (reprinted 1821); revised by George Saintsbury, Edinburgh (1882-92). At present the only complete edition of the *Works.* Chiefly valuable for Scott's *Life* and commentary, a valuable source of information on Restoration England.

2. Editions of Poems, Essays, Plays, etc.

Kinsley, James, ed. *The Poems of John Dryden.* Oxford: Clarendon Press, 1958. 4 vols. A definitive edition.

Ker, W. P., ed. *Essays of John Dryden.* Oxford: Clarendon Press, 1900. 2 vols. (Reprinted New York, 1961). A selection of the most important of Dryden's critical prefaces with spelling modernized; valuable introduction; commentary.

Summers, Montague, ed. *Dryden: The Dramatic Works*. London: The Nonesuch Press, 1932. 6 vols. A complete edition of the plays with notes (highly personal) and introductory material on sources and stage history. Volume I contains a general introduction to Dryden's work as a dramatist.

Ward, Charles E., ed. *The Letters of John Dryden, with Letters Addressed to Him*. Durham, N. C.: Duke University Press, 1942. Sixty-two Dryden letters and fifteen others addressed to him—the sum total of the extant correspondence. Though fragmentary, still helpful in filling in the details of our very partial portrait of the poet.

SECONDARY SOURCES

1. Biographies

Osborn, James. *John Dryden: Some Biographical Facts and Problems*. New York: Columbia University Press, 1940. Valuable to the nonspecialist for its review and assessments of earlier biographies of Dryden. The "problems" considered refer for the most part to minutiae in the poet's life.

Scott, Sir Walter. *Life of Dryden*. The first volume of Scott's edition of Dryden's *Works*. Reprinted and edited for Bison Books by Bernard Kreissman. Lincoln, Nebraska: University of Nebraska Press, 1963. The most sympathetic account and still the clearest picture of the poet.

Saintsbury, George. *Dryden*. New York: Harper and Brothers, n.d. According to Osborne: "The most balanced, the most readable, the most stimulating biography of the great poet that has appeared to this day [1940]."

Ward, Charles E. *The Life of John Dryden*. Chapel Hill, N. C.: University of North Carolina Press, 1961. The most recent and the standard life of Dryden; based upon the most careful judgments of documents and the poet's works.

2. Critical Studies

Aden, John T. "Dryden and the Imagination: The First Phase," *Publications of the Modern Language Association*, LXXIV,

28-40. A detailed study of Dryden's use of the term "Imagination" in his earliest critical writings. The author speaks of continuing his study of the later works in subsequent publication.

Bredvold, Louis. *The Intellectual Milieu of John Dryden. University of Michigan Publications in Language and Literature*, XII. Ann Arbor, Mich.: University of Michigan Press, 1934. A study of the backgrounds of sceptical thought and Anglo-Catholic apologetics relevant to Dryden's religious and political writings. One of the most important works in the Dryden bibliography.

Brower, Reuben. "An Allusion to Europe: Dryden and Tradition," *Alexander Pope: The Poetry of Allusion*. Oxford: Clarendon Press, 1959. Dryden as Pope's teacher in making Homer and Virgil meaningful to the present.

Chambers, A. B. "Absalom and Achitophel: Christ and Satan," *Modern Language Notes*, LXXIV (1959), 592-96. Biblical and Miltonic echoes of Satan's temptation of Christ in *Absalom and Achitophel*.

Chiasson, Elias J. "Dryden's Apparent Scepticism in *Religio Laici*," *Harvard Theological Review*, LIV (1961), 207-221. An argument to substitute an Anglican-Humanist reading for Bredvold's fideist reading of the poem.

Freedman, Morris. "Dryden's Miniature Epic," *Journal of English and Germanic Philology*, LVII, (1958), 211-219. *Absalom and Achitophel* as an epic treatment of Milton's version of the fall of Adam and the temptation of Christ.

Frost, William. *Dryden and the Art of Translation*. New Haven: Yale University Press, 1955. The most extensive treatment of Dryden's theory and practice in translation.

Fujimura, Thomas H. "Dryden's *Religio Laici*: An Anglican Poem," *Publications of the Modern Language Association*, LXXVI (1961), 205-17. A convincing argument to refute Bredvold's reading of the poem as an expression of Dryden's early fideism.

Hartsock, Mildred E. "Dryden's Plays: A Study in Ideas," *Seventeenth Century Studies*, 2nd ser. (ed. Robert Shafer), pp. 71-176. Princeton, N. J.: Princeton University Press, 1937. Chiefly valuable as a collection of references to Hobbesian philosophy in Dryden's plays.

Hooker, Edward N. "Dryden and the Atoms of Epicurus," *English Literary History*, XXIV (1957), 177-90. Argues that Dryden's scepticism in *Religio Laici* is the mean between the two extremes of dogmatism and Pyrrhonism.

————. "The Purpose of Dryden's *Annus Mirabilis*" *Huntington Library Quarterly*, X (1946), 49-67. An interpretation of the poem as a work of Tory propaganda opposing Puritan attempts to read the events of 1666 as evidence of God's anger at the restoration of Charles II.

Huntley, Frank L. *On Dryden's "Essay of Dramatic Poesy" University of Michigan Contributions in Modern Philology*, No. 16. Ann Arbor, Mich.: University of Michigan Press, 1951. A line-by-line analysis of the *Essay*, revealing the structural pattern of Dryden's critical thought.

Jones, Richard F. "The Originality of *Absalom and Achitophel*," *Modern Language Notes*, XLVI (1931), 211-18. A survey of the applications of the Absalom and Achitophel story to the seventeenth-century political situation: hence, an essay on the *un*originality of Dryden's poem.

Kirsch, Arthur C. "The Significance of Dryden's *Aureng-Zebe*," *English Literary History*, XXIX (1962), 160-74. An analysis of the play as an anticipation of sentimental tragedy.

King, Bruce. "Dryden's Intent in *All for Love*," *College English*, XXIV (1963), 266-70. On interpretation of the play in the light of the tragic theories of Rapin and Rymer.

————. "*Don Sebastian*: Dryden's Moral Fable," *Sewanee Review*, LXX (1962), 651-70. A reinterpretation of Dryden's conception of "moral" as symbol with respect to Dryden's "best play."

McKeithan, David M. "The Occasion of *Mac Flecknoe*," *Publications of the Modern Language Association*, XLVII (1932), 766-71. A survey of the Dryden-Shadwell quarrel prior to the pirated publication of *Mac Flecknoe*.

Roper, Alan H. "Dryden's *Medal* and the Divine Analogy," *English Literary History*, XXIX (1962), 396-417. An application of the "conservative myth" to *The Medall*.

Schilling, Bernard N. *Dryden and the Conservative Myth: A Reading of Absalom and Achitophel.* New Haven: Yale University Press, 1961. A line-by-line analysis of the poem in terms of Restoration conservatism: the Variorum *Absalom and Achitophel.*

Tanner, J. E. "The Messianic Image in *Mac Flecknoe*," *Modern Language Notes*, LXXVI 220-23. The "divine analogy" applied to literary satire: Shadwell as Christ.

Trowbridge, Hoyt. "The Place of the Rules in Dryden's Criticism," *Modern Philology*, XLIV (1946), 84-96. Defines Dryden's sceptical attitude in criticism as "probabilism." An important contribution.

Van Doren, Mark. *The Poetry of John Dryden.* New York: Harcourt, Brace & World, Inc., 1920. The best critical estimate of Dryden's nondramatic verse.

Wallerstein, Ruth C. "To Madness Near Allied: Shaftesbury and His Place in the Design and Thought of *Absalom and Achitophel*," *Huntington Library Quarterly*, VI (1943), 445-71. A study of Dryden's use of the "humour" psychology in his portrait of Achitophel.

————. "'On the Death of Mrs. Killigrew: The Perfecting of a Genre," *Studies in Philology*, XLIV (1947), 519-28. A comparison of the Killegrew ode and the elegy to Lord Hastings as illustration of Dryden's mastery of the conventions of the elegy.

Wasserman, Earl. "Dryden: Epistle to Charleton," *The Subtler Language.* Baltimore: The Johns Hopkins Press, 1959. An analysis of the poem in terms of Dryden's poetic use of the idea of the Restoration.

————. "Pope's *Ode for Musick*," *English Literary History*, XXVIII (1961), 163-86. A brilliant analysis of the metrical structure and effects of Dryden's Song for St. Cecilia's Day."

Williamson, George. "The Occasion of An Essay of Dramatic Poesy," *Modern Philology*, XLIV (1946), 1-9. Considers the *Essay* as an answer to Sorbière's *Voyage to England.*

————. *The Proper Wit of Poetry.* Chicago: University of Chicago Press, 1961. A study of Dryden's changing conception of "wit."

Index